WE LEAD

HOW WOMEN BECOME LEADERS

We lead: how women become leaders

Published by Novaro Publishing Ltd, Techno Centre, Coventry University Technology Park, Puma Way, Coventry CV1 2TT e: publish@novaropublishing.com. www.novaropublishing.com

ISBN: 978-1-9998329-4-0

A CIP catalogue record for this book is available from the British Library.

Designed and typeset by Kate Wiliwinska / Lawston Design. Cover by Chantel Barrett at Clear Design.

WE LEAD

HOW WOMEN BECOME LEADERS

HILARIE OWEN

NOVARO PUBLISHING

HILARIE OWEN is an authority on what makes great leaders and how top teams excel. She has worked for global companies and two government departments, as well as with the RAF Red Arrows and Harvard University. She has resolved leadership challenges in many different countries and is in regular demand as a keynote speaker. She is recognised as an expert for her research on how leadership is learnt, the crossovers with neuroscience and how decisions are made. Alongside her work in mentoring senior directors and top teams, Hilarie has launched a programme for women who are aiming to take up leadership roles. This is her ninth book on leadership.

CONTENTS

To Riley and Theo
who bring joy and pride

FOREWORD

Brian Patterson, executive and leadership coach, Praesta, and former chairman, The Irish Times

---

The journey towards women's empowerment and respect for them as leaders has been a long one. There have been many important steps along the way – winning the right to vote, equality legislation, training and development initiatives – and more recently the #MeToo movement. All of these stepping stones are critically necessary preconditions, but of themselves they haven't resulted in enough women leaders. We're not there yet.

Women who have made the final push into positions of senior leadership have often had to do so by mimicking the attitudes, the behaviour and even the dress of men. In doing so, they may have lost that different quality that women bring to the leadership of organizations and communities. In some cases, they have even unconsciously adopted some of the dysfunctional behaviours of men. Often, they also had to compromise their traditional roles as mothers and daughters, roles that hold our societies together.

But it need not be so. For there is a growing number of women who have made it into positions of leadership without losing their authentically female perspective and who have found ways of maintaining their familial roles. Quietly practicing elements of servant leadership, they avoid becoming the ego-based leader as hero and so they have no need for the limelight. Many people are consequently unaware of the number of women who are already leading large, complex organizations. This book brings those women into our view and helps us understand their personal journeys and how they have emerged as authentically female leaders, each expressing her own unique personality, set of values and style of leadership.

There's now evidence that boards and leadership teams with a good gender balance bring about better and more sustainable results. But there is still some way to go before that balance becomes more widespread.

For 20 years, Hilarie Owen has been at the forefront of understanding leadership and, in particular, how individuals build their unique leader capability. She has often been ahead of others in her groundbreaking work with individuals and organizations. This book will help to increase the number of women in leadership roles by illuminating the pathway for the next generations of women leaders. It deserves to be read by women who aspire to become leaders – and those who already are. Men could learn a lot from it too.

PREFACE

Most organizations are aware of gender inequality and many are trying to address the issue with training programmes, coaching and building a pipeline of talent, but these actions are not delivering the results quickly enough. Filling the pipeline hasn't produced the results and neither have policies. The barriers that hinder progress for women are far more complex and elusive.

It took many years of action to enable women to be where they are today. We should never forget those brave women and men who campaigned, fought and died for women to have an equal place in the world. As a milestone, 2018 has been important for not only was it a hundred years since the first women in the UK had the vote but the #MeToo campaign raised awareness of how women are still perceived by some men.

Following my webinar on women, power and leadership that was held on International Women's Day 2018 with three great speakers, I decided to explore women leaders in more depth. I interviewed women leaders across society from business, the arts, science, sport, technology and government. I was enthralled by their autobiographical narratives. Their stories were engaging and it became clear that their leadership emerged and grew from their continual learning and experiences. It quickly unfolded that there were key patterns that were central to their ability to lead that I will try and capture in this book.

Each woman, regardless of their differences, background or education, had common elements they had developed. It wasn't as simple as qualities, as important as these are, but constructs they had combined to form their leadership – a different form of leadership to the older male version. Each expressed their leadership differently, for there is no single model or theory, but a collage. Yet what made up that collage had similarities. Where leadership goes wrong in organizations is that so many try and put leadership in a box, label it and transport it into courses. It doesn't work. The aim here is to show a different approach that I will outline at the end of the book.

The book consists of four main parts but begins with the context in which women have to work. It clarifies the challenges they face that men do not. We need men to understand and work with us to change things. The first part explores how women construct their identity as a leader and who influences this. The second part is on how women leaders build credibility and the key elements that make this effective. The third part addresses the courage required which is an essential part of leadership. Finally, the fourth part clarifies what organizations need to do to create and sustain the right culture so all who have the potential to become leaders can express it for the benefit of others and the organization. It also includes a route map that will help individual women become a leader.

Much has been written on leadership, particularly from the US, so I wanted this work to be more British. Being Welsh, I had reasons for also wanting this work to include Celtic women. Therefore I focused on women leaders from Wales, Ireland, Scotland and England across sectors in working life. My reason wasn't egotistical but historical.

In the past, Celtic women were often leaders until Roman and then Germanic invasions. In fact, the Roman historian Tacitus (AD56-117) wrote that Celtic women were by no means excluded from positions of authority. More recently, in 1979 Margaret O' Hara and Bernadette Bulfin wrote about the ancient laws of Ireland and Wales:

> They gave more rights and protection to women than any other Western law code at that time or since. Equal pay for work of equal value, protection from violence, equitable separation laws, enforcement during marriage of the right of both spouses to respect and fidelity was the norm before the conquests.

However, we must not believe this was a perfect world for Celt society. We have to put this into the context of the time when life was hard for most. Having said that, the reality was that Celtic women could govern, took prominent roles in political, religious and artistic life; became judges and lawgivers, they could own property which marriage could not deprive them of; they could choose when they wanted to marry and, often, to whom; they could divorce, and, if they were deserted, maltreated or molested, they had the right to claim considerable damages. This disappeared first with Roman occupation, then Saxon and Norman, but also with the influence of western Christianity, with its Greek and Roman codes that transformed Celtic society.

The fact that Celtic women were leaders is part of history. Perhaps the most well-known is Boudica of the first century AD. She was ruler of her people and accepted as a war leader by her own and other neighbouring tribes. In history, we are told about the speech Tudor Queen Elizabeth I is supposed to have given to the troops at Tilbury in 1588 (Elizabeth was a descendent of the daughter of Llewelyn Fawr, Prince of Wales) but not so many know of the speech Boudica gave from her war chariot facing the Roman army. Agricola, the father-in-law of Tacitus, witnessed the battle and later recorded her words as:

> I do not come to boast the pride of my ancestry, not even to recover the plundered wealth of my family. I take the field like the ordinary citizens among you, to assert the cause of liberty; to seek justice for my body, scarred with the Roman lash, and to avenge my raped daughters. From the pride and arrogance of Rome, nothing is sacred; all are subject to violation; the old endure the whip and the young girls are raped.

For Celtic women, fairness was important as was justice and they were as strong a leader as any man. It isn't fair that women earn less than men and it isn't fair that men dominate top positions. In Celtic society, it was important to retain an order in which women were balanced in relation to men. From Cornwall and Breton to Ireland, Wales and

Scotland, women saw society transform and today they have a key role in its transformation again along with their equals in England.

Meeting and interviewing women leaders has been enlightening and inspiring. When women have power and leadership, what can we learn from them? In all the interviews I did not meet one giant ego or 'performance'. The women were open, authentic and wanted to show a path for others to follow or help them find their own leadership way.

Having studied, researched and practiced leadership for over 20 years, I wanted to capture the learning from each of the interviews and share it. So often we hear that there are not enough female role models. My experience is that they are there if you look and when you find them they are often no different from you and me. They are certainly organized and have support around them, for it is still a hazardous road, but I believe the world will be better placed when more women lead. One day when someone asks women 'what do you do?'. The answer will be 'we lead'.

Hilarie Owen,
January 2019

1.
CONTEXT

In the last 25 years women have entered the professional and managerial ranks at the same rate as men yet remain under-represented at senior levels. This is a pervasive issue as female talent, power and opportunity are underused around the world. Yet women today control at least 20 percent of the world's wealth according to the Centre for Talent Innovation. In addition, a 2016 report published by Credit Suisse is typical of several research studies in finding companies that employ women in large numbers and have at least three women on their board outperform their competitors on every measure of profitability. However, there is a danger in just relying on numbers as an indicator. Other factors also influence company performance such as having the right culture in organizations.

Women are making inroads but we don't always know or hear about it. That is why this book needed to be written. While the numbers are too few and another generation of young women are saying, 'there are no female role models', I want to show that there are women doing amazing things. I believe there is a 'quiet revolution' going on as more women take up leadership roles across society and I would like to share some of their stories and thoughts with you.

Building on my own research over 20 years into how individuals actually learn leadership, I wanted to write this book specifically on women leaders. Finding the women was so easy it seemed that synchronicity was at play where something other than the probability of chance was involved. I had a list of questions to ask, 15 in all, to use as a basis of interviews. I stopped at 30 women but could have gone on. I wanted women from a range of sectors but had no preconceptions of what would emerge. Each person was asked the same questions and early on patterns began to emerge that were unexpected. Most of the women leaders had children but not all. Most had experienced failure or a difficult challenge and it was interesting to hear how they dealt with that. What emerged were real women who had become leaders in their own right with a depth of experience that could inspire others to follow. Here are the women who were interviewed.

Introducing the women leaders

- **Anne Jessopp** is the first female chief executive of the Royal Mint owned by the Treasury.

- **Dr Alice Bunn** is director of the UK Space Agency, which manages civil space programmes for the UK government.

- **Air Vice-Marshal Sue Gray** is chief engineer of the RAF, also lead of infrastructure through 38 Group that employs 3000 people. She was twice deployed to Iraq.

- **Diane Savory OBE** was chief operating officer for Cult Clothing that became Superdry, a clothes brand trading in 38 countries. Today she chairs several organizations.

- **Paula Martin** is chief executive of the Cornwall Air Ambulance Trust and chairs the Association of Air Ambulances.

- **Donna Baddeley** is chief executive of Valleys to Coast Housing Ltd, helping people in South Wales find homes.

- **Chief Constable Sara Thornton CBE QPM** is chair of the national police chiefs' council and was a former chief constable of Thames Valley Police

- **Jo Miller** is chief executive of Doncaster Council and recognized as an inspiring leader in local government.

- **Jeanette Forbes**, a qualified system engineer, is the founder and chief executive of PLC Group, which serves the offshore, marine, commercial, industrial and renewables sectors.

- **Ann Compton** is former senior partner at Rickerbys, a firm of solicitors.

- **Dara Deering** is executive director of retail banking at KBC Bank Ireland.

- **Fiona Clark**, now head of English at the Rashid School for Boys, began her career in communications for the Design Council and the National Trust.

- **Sacha Romanovitch** was the first female chief executive of a major accountancy firm, Grant Thornton.

- **Ann Daniels** is a polar explorer, who was one of the first women to reach both the North Pole and South Pole

- **Rebecca Evernden** is director of the UK Space Agency, working with government ministers. She is an expert in climate change adaptation and shares her job with Alice Bunn.

- **Camilla Stowell** is managing director and head of wealth and investment at Coutts International.

- **Sheila Richards** was previous general manager at Nuffield Hospital and spent ten years working for the NHS across the UK

- **Jenny Tooth OBE** is chief executive of the UK Business Angels Association, who has huge experience of working with the EU

- **Baroness Tanni Grey Thompson** is a Paralympian champion with over 35 world records and now sits in the House of Lords.

- **Katherine Bennett OBE** is senior vice-president at Airbus responsible for over 10,000 people. She is a fellow of the Royal Aeronautical Society.

- **Lisa Marie Brown** is founder and managing director of

Pinkspiration, a construction business that helps young people develop skills to transform empty spaces in communities.

- **Jackie Royall** is managing director at Viscose Closures Ltd and a board member of the Family Housing Association (Wales), who is a qualified accountant and turnaround consultant.

- **Kully Thiarai**, director of National Theatre Wales, has many years' experience nationally and internationally in performing arts, commissioning, producing and directing.

- **Fiona Driscoll** is an experienced chief executive of global companies and is now a non-executive director of UK Research & Innovation and on the board of the Nuffield Trust.

- **Dr Rabinder Buttar** is chief executive and chair of Clintec International, a global clinical research organization for the biotech, pharma and medical-device industries

- **Nicola Henderson** came second in the Clipper Round the World Race as the youngest ever skipper.

- **Linda Green** is chief executive of Linda's Inns, who has huge experience in the retail and hospitality sectors.

- **Jane Hutt AM** is deputy minister in the office of the first minister and chief whip at the Welsh Assembly.

- **Cheryl Haswell** is matron at two leading hospitals, the Dilke and the Lydney.

- **Emma Hall** is a chartered financial planner and a fellow of the Personal Finance Authority.

Each of these women had a unique leadership story. Their intelligence, attention to detail and inspiring stories can now show a path for others. The key question is how do women become leaders across society? We know that around the world today more women are highly educated than men and are just as ambitious. The problem isn't women but organizations and society which still propagate stereotypes. So how do women break through these and what do organizations need to do to ensure the talent of women is not wasted in a world that requires the best leaders?

Equality is certainly taking a long time to reach. Research, both nationally, such as reports from the Cranfield School of Management, and internationally, including the World Economic Forum, say it will take longer than previously expected suggesting around 180 more years. But we are where we are and the starting place is to begin by clarifying the context in which change has to occur.

Year for women

Many of us ended up calling 2018 'the year for women'. Although the momentum will have to continue for lasting change, there were three events that together created an awareness of how women's lives have changed and how we have to continue to improve the lives of all women and men.

First, it was the hundredth anniversary of the first British women to have the vote after a hard and long battle with its martyrs and heroines. It even had its own battle song:

'Rise up women, for the fight is hard and long;
Rise in thousands singing loud a battle song.'

Written by Theodora Mills and sung to the tune of
John Brown's Body

Changing people's beliefs was indeed a hard battle as this comment shows: 'the participation of women in politics was, as every decent woman knew, unnatural, and those who pressed for it were simply psychological misfits', said Sir Almoth Wright in 1912.

As the franchise movement gathered strength those opposing women's suffrage, including women, had their own songs too:

'Little Jill Horner
Sulks in the corner
What is the reason why?
She says she'll be glum
Till she gets a thumb
And a finger in every pie.'

Yet the battle didn't finish when all women won the vote. In the 1950s, Maurice Duverger would comment: 'while women have legally ceased to be minors, they still have the mentality of minors in many fields and particularly in politics'.

Resistance to having fingers in pies is still prevalent today. Recently some viewers criticized the BBC for having so many women in positions of authority in its series *The Bodyguard*. The response was even more aggressive to the BBC's new lunchtime politics programme, *Politics Live*, when the panel of MPs and journalists on the first day happened to be all women. Tweets from both men and women called for someone to be sacked. How often do we see male-only conversations on politics or business with no response?

This backlash is sometimes called 'centrality' and operates when men feel it is a right or entitlement to hold a privileged place including leadership in the home, at work, in politics and in society. It is the loss of this privilege that produces grievance.

The Geena Davis Institute on Gender in Media found that when a room has 20 percent women, men perceive this as 50 percent. Above 20 percent, the feeling men then experience is that women are taking over. This happens with young school pupils too. A study by the American Council on Education asked teachers to tell pupils to fill a room with 50 percent girls and 50 percent boys. The boys were asked how they felt afterwards and the most common response was: 'the girls are getting all the attention'. Many boys and men feel a loss when equality is achieved. Their view of centrality is threatened because they have normalized balance in their favour and therefore equality is disruptive. This is why most policies are ineffective and why so few men take up the issue of gender balance.

When looking at women's representation in politics, newer governments seem to do more to include women in their legislatures compared to countries with older institutions. Following the 2014 election in South Africa, women occupied 42.4 percent of the parliamentary seats. In Mexico, women occupy 47.8 percent of the lower house seats and 49.2 percent of the senate. In Rwanda, more than 61 percent take their seats in their house and 38.5 percent in the senate. While daily life is hard for women in Rwanda, the pay gap for women is lower than the US. In Cuba, 53.2 percent are women in their parliament, while in Bolivia 53.1 percent of women are in the house and 47.2 percent in the senate. In Granada, 46.7 percent of women are in the house and in Namibia 46 percent in the house. In comparison, the US is ranked 102nd in the world with just 19.5 percent of women in the house and 22 percent in the senate, while China is ranked 70th with around 25 percent of its legislative seats occupied by women. At present in the UK, there are 208 women MPs in the House of Commons, which is 32 percent, but the top cabinet posts are men apart from the prime minister who has been on shaky ground for a long time. In the House of Lords, women peers make up 26 percent of the numbers.

Do women in politics make a difference to people's lives? When women politicians rose in number in the UK, they put forward a bill on violence against women. In Bolivia they have worked on a bill against violence against women in politics. With the huge rise of this issue with female politicians here in the UK, it is worth noting that there are still those who do not want women to have fingers in pies including politics. During the Brexit negotiations there have been disgraceful comments from Tory MPs aimed at the prime minister including the worst from an unnamed one who cowardly wrote: 'the moment is coming when the knife gets heated, stuck in her front and twisted. She'll be dead soon'.

There still remain obstacles, particularly in countries with a long history of institutions designed by men. One of which is regarding female candidates as a lame duck. However, research shows that when women stand for election, they have an equal chance of succeeding as male candidates and seem to work harder while in office. As political parties and constituencies become more accountable and more transparent, more doors will open for women.

Global gender gap

The second event of 2018 was the publication of *The Global Gender Gap Report* by the World Economic Forum, highlighting progress for women in education across the world: more young women are now having a university education than young men, although it is still not reflected in the workplace or politics. Fewer women are hired at entry level and around one in five C-suite leaders globally are women.

In the workplace, the evidence consistently suggests that women on boards leads to better performance and wider recruitment. However, the issue has turned into a numbers game. FTSE companies have the odd one or two non-executives on their boards, rather than full-time executives. The Cranfield School of Management has been monitoring senior appointments by FTSE companies for many years. Its 2018 report warns that the large companies face an acute shortage of female executives ready to step up to chair their boards after repeatedly failing to increase the number of women holding the most senior roles.

Only 9.7 percent of full-time executives on FTSE 100 boards are women and 2018 is the fourth consecutive year in which the figure has flatlined. More positively, the overall percentage of women on FTSE 100 boards increased to 29 percent. However, this increase was driven by women being appointed to non-executive roles, rather than promotions to the executive ranks. Many of these non-executives on one board were on other boards too.

Further down, the picture is worse. The number of female executive directors in the FTSE 250 dropped from 38 to 30 the Cranfield report found, while the overall number of women on boards increased only slightly to 23.7 percent.

When looking at the context, it is worth noting that we've had 20 years of talent pipelines and other HR initiatives that have changed little. With the threat of government legislation, there have been some positive steps in the UK but not enough. Recently, the government threatened not to approve new executives at the Bank of England, as no women were being appointed.

The Hampton-Alexander review, backed by the government, is monitoring progress, including FTSE 350 chairs and chief executives. What's so startling are the reasons for slow progress, even though there is a target of a third of women board members by 2020. In the findings released by the Department for Business, Energy and Industrial Strategy in May 2018, it quoted the following comments it had received:

- 'I don't think women fit comfortably into the board environment.'

- 'There aren't that many women with the right credentials and depth of experience to sit on the board – the issues covered are extremely complex.'

- 'Shareholders just aren't interested in the make-up of the board, so why should we be?'

- 'My other board colleagues wouldn't want to appoint a woman to the board.'

- 'All the "good" women have been snapped up.'

- 'We have one woman already on the board, so we are done – it is someone else's turn.'

Yet some researchers argue, in particular McKinsey's annual report, *Diversity Matters*, that our most successful companies are those that champion diversity and have at least two women on their boards. This would also go some way towards addressing the gender pay gap. Many companies reported that this was due to insufficient women in senior roles. In addition, research by McKinsey from their *UK Gender Pay Gap Report: 2018* states that bridging the gender pay gap could add £150bn to the UK economy by 2025 and this would translate into 840,000 additional female employees.

However, according to the World Economic Forum the pay gap will not be closed until 2235 if the current rate of change continues.

In the UK, the Office for National Statistics reports that 3.8 million or 28 percent of all jobs done by women are paid below the living wage compared to 20 percent of men. Finally, according to the Young Women's Trust, one in ten HR decision-makers in organizations with more than 250 employees are aware of women in their organization being paid less than men for jobs at the same level.

Companies are trying to address gender issues by offering mentoring schemes and networks specifically targeted at women. The highest number of companies that provide this are the US (88 percent), France (75 percent) and the UK (71 percent) and yet other countries are more successful in promoting women into leadership roles. Therefore what barriers are preventing more women leaders? Why is it so hard for women to achieve top leadership positions in big companies? In particular, why can't companies today include women in the executive ranks? *The Global Gender Gap Report* found in their survey across the world that the biggest barriers were:

- General norms and cultural practices in the countries

- Masculine/patriarchal corporate culture

- Lack of role models

Whereas the least important in the survey were:

- Lack of adequate parental leave and benefits

- Inadequate labour laws and regulations

In other words, policies only go so far but the issue is one of the culture and the behaviours that are resulting in low numbers of senior women in the workplace.

Another issue is how organizations develop women leaders and track careers. An article in *Harvard Business Review* by Hewlett and Luce (2005) opened people's eyes to how different women's careers tend to be compared to men's. They described it as 'off ramps and on ramps' as women progress, taking time off to address other aspects of their lives including having children. The women interviewed for this book took maternity leave, but some felt pressure to return as soon as possible.

Addressing the working lives of parents has to change as the millennials have grown up in an era where diversity, the gig economy and the desire for a work-life balance are the norm for both women and men.

Another study, *Benefits of Multiple Roles for Managerial Women* by Ruderman and Ohlott from the Centre for Creative Leadership (2002), goes as far as to say conventional careers, based on the experience of married men, do not readily apply to women. The old model is certainly changing as both mothers and fathers want time for children and some fathers are taking over as the main parent. However, the most striking part of the Ruderman and Ohlott study of 61 female high achievers was the developmental expectation of the women. These were:

- Authenticity – wanting to align inner values and beliefs and outer behaviours.

- Connection – to feel close and attached to others.

- Control of one's own destiny – to act for oneself to influence the environment around them.

- Self-clarity – to understand their strengths and weaknesses, motives and behaviours.

- Wholeness – the ability to integrate the personal and professional life goals.

As you read this book, you will see that these development issues were also present in the women leaders interviewed here. They talk about their values and being authentic; how they prefer to walk around their building than be stuck up on the top floor; they were very self-aware and use their strengths to influence the culture and take time for outside the workplace whether it was doing sport or being with the family. They were also aware of the support from their partners and families in enabling them to have their careers.

What is clear is that gender parity is not a woman's problem but a societal one that requires a global solution by organizations in all sectors including the glamourous world of show business.

Societal issues

The third event, and possibly the most high profile, was the exposure of movie mogul Harvey Weinstein, accused of rape and sexual assault by the actor Emma Loman. To accuse any man with power and money would be difficult but what happened next was a game changer. The use of the hashtag #MeToo by the social activist Tarana Burke was picked up by the actor Alyssa Milano on Twitter to raise the issue of sexual harassment and assault that spread virally on social media. Others were encouraged to join the campaign, including Gwyneth Paltrow, Jennifer Lawrence, Uma Thurman and Debra Messing. Then it spread across society, including the church, politics and sport, and to countries as diverse as Australia, Canada, Afghanistan, India and even China, although the state has tried to suppress it.

What it all reflects is how men have controlled power and how women have remained silent for years because they don't think the police or law will believe them. As Baroness Helena Kennedy argued at The Times Literature Festival in 2018, the law is letting women down. These system failures have made it difficult for girls and women to have enough trust in it to speak up. Change should now happen, although, if it is to last, we have to address the concept of power.

For International Women's Day 2018, I organized a webinar on redefining power and leadership with three guest speakers: Professor Dacher Keltner, who I heard speak at Davos in 2018 and read his book *The Power Paradox*; Leslie Abdela MBE who set up the 300 Group in 1980 to get more women into parliament and politics; and Georgia Williams an officer in the RAF whose research on masculinity has interesting conclusions that includes how women leaders may regard other women who are not leaders. The discussion showed how complex the issue is and the hard work still required for parity.

The paradox that Dacher talks about is that the seduction of power induces people to lose the skills that enabled them to gain it in the first place. He shows through research that people who feel powerful are more likely to act impulsively, have affairs, lie and justify their rule-breaking and even steal when wealthy. Think of people who fit this and you will see someone who has built a power base around themselves to feel powerful. To replace this, Dacher says power can be redefined as serving good and making a difference in the world by focusing on other people and taking delight in what others can achieve. To make this change the role of leaders is to create an environment or culture where others can succeed.

The 2018 Grant Thornton *Women in Business* report, a global study of business leaders and progress on gender diversity, found there was far too much focus on ticking boxes rather than creating a culture that would harness genuinely diverse senior management teams. In other words, while policies were in place such as equal pay, flexible hours and paid parental leave, they found that businesses that have the most policies are not necessarily those that demonstrate good gender diversity. Policies in businesses in the UK are already there, such as ones to attract and keep employees (82 percent) and policies to live up to organizational values (82 percent). Therefore policies alone, while as good as they are, do not create the necessary progress that is required.

In fact, stereotypes about gender roles are still a barrier, which governments try to address through policies. Again, these are not resulting in large-scale change and are not enough alone. However, the Grant Thornton study did find real change when policies and practices are rooted in genuine conviction of the benefits of diversity from the most senior leaders who then drove inclusive cultures. Therefore, we don't need any more policies but, rather, leaders to champion the cause of gender diversity. This includes more men to be involved as Emma Watson argues for the UN's He for She campaign. From a mix of recent reports on gender in the UK the following highlights can be made:

- There are more than 2 million women working in management in the UK.

- They feel there is a lack of female role models in top positions to inspire them.

- 43 percent of middle female managers feel they are likely to leave their current employer in the next two years. The reasons are lack of opportunities (48 percent), poor likelihood of progression (47 percent) and lack clarity of career path (40 percent).

- Blocked female talent is losing the UK £5bn a year.

- Companies that employ female senior managers have shareholder returns on average 53 percent higher and profit margins 42 percent better where at least one in three board members are female.

These economic points show that parity is not just about fairness. If you count how many purchasing decisions women make and how much their priorities determine household finances, their influence is substantial.

Globally, the picture is encouraging with progress on the number of businesses with women in senior management primarily driven by emerging economies such as Africa where 89 percent have at least one woman in senior management, Eastern Europe at 87 percent and Latin America at 65 percent.

Is the problem with the UK and US that our old institutions are holding back parity in our society? Is it that those in power feel they have more to lose than gain? One of those sectors is the judiciary. Lady Hale, the first female president of the UK Supreme Court, argues for more diversity so the public can feel that it is 'their judges' in court and not 'beings from another planet'. In *The Guardian* on 1st January 2019, she said that the law needs the different perspectives and experiences that diversity brings.

In addition, the Grant Thornton report found that initiatives to 'fix' women into the existing ways that businesses operate miss an opportunity. When the focus is creating an inclusive culture based around shared purpose and collaboration, real change occurs. What is interesting was that many of the women leaders interviewed here knew that and were working to achieve it, not just for women, but for everyone. Therefore women leaders are not just role models, they are also change makers. However, not all change is valued and women can still find themselves isolated.

Numerous studies have confirmed that reducing gender inequality enhances productivity and economic growth. In the developed countries, the boost to GDP would be 9 percent in the US, 1.3 percent in the eurozone and 16 percent in Japan, according to the World Economic Forum.

Accelerating change

This context affects not only women but men and the whole of society. Change depends on us all, starting with those who have power and influence. In January 2018, leaders at the World Economic Forum committed themselves to a fresh series of efforts. The prime minister of Canada, Justin Trudeau, stood up and said:

> I'd like to focus on a fundamental shift that every leader in this room can act on immediately, one that I have made a central tenet of my leadership. I'm talking about hiring, promoting and retaining more women….. and not just because it's the right thing to do, or the nice thing to do, but because it's the smart thing to do.

Trudeau then added figures to demonstrate that gender parity would add $1.75 trillion to the GDP of the US and $2.5 trillion to China's. In Canada, he said closing the gender gap could result in $150bn more output by 2026.

His government has set up a Gender Equality Advisory Council to co-ordinate activities and outcomes during Canada's presidency of the G7. The council is led by Melinda Gates, Isabelle Hudson, who is Canada's ambassador to France, and Malala Yousafzai, winner of the Nobel Peace Prize. Already things are changing, as Canada has as many women as men in its cabinet and has introduced a gender-responsive national budget.

The G7 stated that gender equality was a human right and top priority, producing a document, *Roadmap for a Gender-Responsive Economic Environment*, which pledges to increase women's participation and leadership in all walks of life, promoting female entrepreneurship, improving women's access to jobs and equal pay, and stopping violence against girls and women.

Next year, France takes up the presidency of the G7. Already President Emmanuel Macron has given women crucial cabinet posts and helped increase the number of women in the lower house of parliament, as well as introducing measures on equal pay, sexual harassment and violence against women.

Such positive measures are happening within the context of the turmoil that we are all experiencing following the financial crash and Brexit. So, if we take a group of women leaders from across organizations, what can we learn about meeting these objectives in practice and realizing the potential for leadership in our own lives?

The aim of this book is to inspire a wide audience to take up this leadership challenge. These interviews give those who want to follow these 30 women to the top a template and a set of guidelines. We begin by exploring how women develop their leadership skills and question the present ways in which organizations currently support them.

PART 1:
CONSTRUCT

You've just had a memo from the HR department saying that leadership development is a priority for the next six months and that you have to attend a week's course at a top business school in the Lake District next month. How do you feel about it?

This scenario happens in organizations every day. What hasn't been realised is that learning and developing leadership is not achieved on a training course or coaching – no matter how good or how much fun. Developing your leadership is a lifelong process. It began before you went to school and will continue indefinitely.

Our tendency in life today is to look for the quick fix and we assume the problem is with people when in fact often it is with the organization. Leadership is as much about who you are as what you do and how you do it. The process is ongoing and it's never too late or too early to begin. The key is being open to learning from all experience.

Leadership involves thinking, feeling, perception and behaviour. These thoughts and feelings are based on past and present events and experiences, making leadership a personal expression of the way one relates to the world. The mistake made by many is the belief that a single model or tool will create a similar result in everyone. Leadership cannot be put in a box, though many have tried. Try and see leadership as a journey that you take to a place not yet experienced.

Like a journey, leadership does not happen in isolation. It is a dynamic and active journey between ourselves, others and the world. In other words, leadership is a social construct. As such, it puts together different parts to form something whole. We are not born a leader, but grow into leadership through combining and arranging these different parts. In this study of women leaders, it was clear that leadership is something they grew into and it began in childhood. The influence of childhood on these women was so significant we need to explore it as it seems, this is where all leadership begins.

2.

AFFIRMATION

The question everyone asks is: are leaders born or made? The answer is they are made and it begins in early childhood. What we know is that from the age of two to three, children begin to understand that there are two genders and start to pick up on the rules about what each should do and what is typical behaviour. Children then apply these rules to themselves and what they do. This includes the rules for leaders and leadership.

In my leadership research with 5-18-year-olds over three years (*Creating Leaders in the Classroom*, Routledge, 2007) I found that 5-6-year-olds have a wide spectrum of who is a leader but this narrows as they grow older with an emphasis on positional leaders coming from the influence of the media and society. At six, their choice of leader was influenced by gender with girls saying 'my sister' or 'the queen' can be a leader whereas boys said 'a soldier' or 'a footballer'. The research also found that children begin to differentiate between 'leader' and 'leadership'.

By age ten they were clear that a leader was 'older, bigger, bossier and cleverer than me'. This was the construct for many and it had a huge impact on seeing themselves as a leader. They believed that because I'm not like what a leader should be, I can't be a leader. In other words, if I'm not older, bigger, bossier and cleverer, then I can't be a leader. This belief is known as an implicit leadership theory. Yet when they described leadership it included 'being good, not being bossy, helping others, sharing and doing everything right'. In other words there was a clear distinction between a leader and leadership. This continued throughout the age groups.

When the youngsters were asked who was a leadership role model, the majority said a parent. To the question can leadership be learned 89 percent said 'yes'. Then came their views of each other as leaders and gender stereotyping was apparent. Girls describing how boys lead included:

> Boys are tougher. Boys want to start a war. Girls stick at things and stop and think. Boys go straight into action. Boys fight. Girls try to reason. Boys always think of themselves and not others. Girls try to make friends with the group they are leading, while boys just get on with it. Girls work as a team whereas boys tend to take it on by themselves. Girls think more and are calmer. Girls are more reliable.

Boys said:

> Boys like action, girls are more into appearance. Girls are bossier, boys are stronger. Boys will get in a fight, girls use words. Boys follow one, girls decide in groups. Boys are braver and more competitive, girls are less confident. Boys are more direct, girls think more. Boys take risks, girls lead more subtly. Girls are wimps.

These differences were also found when asked what qualities were the most important for a leader.

For the girls:

- Kind to others: 40 percent
- Confidence: 24 percent
- Listen to others: 18 percent
- Take responsibility: 16 percent

For the boys:

- Confidence: 37 percent
- To be strong: 34 percent
- To have courage: 16 percent
- To be helpful: 13 percent

As Warren Bennis, the late distinguished professor of leadership, wrote in *On Becoming a Leader Revised* (2003):

> By the time we reach puberty, the world has reached us and shaped us to a greater extent than we realise. Our family, friends, school and society in general have told us – by word and example – how to be. But people begin to become leaders at that moment when they decide for themselves how to be.

This is why our childhood is so powerful in how it shapes us and how prevalent stereotypes are. A recent study of 2000 people in the UK found gender stereotyping and discrimination was limiting both women and men in their career choices and found nearly 40 percent of the UK population steeped in gender stereotyping.

Finally, in the three-year youth study, when asked for examples of leaders in their classroom there was a difference in who they chose. For example, they said: 'Hannah because she's smart and kind'. Whereas they said: 'James because he's in charge of the football team'. They were choosing two leaders based on different criteria. The girl was judged by her behaviour and the boy was judged by what he did.

Ex-teacher Nancy Kline explained this in her book, *Women and Power: How Far Can We Go?* (1993):

> Women are taught from their earliest years that their excellence as women will be judged by the way they interact with people and whether or not people flourish in their care. Men are taught that their excellence as men will be judged by the way they control people and how

well they promote themselves and by whether or not they stay 'on top'.

Kline goes on to say that men go on to think in terms of win or lose, whilst women think interactively with and about people: these two messages result in two different kinds of leaders. It is worth noting that some of the boys in the youth study remarked that they preferred how the girls lead.

The world has changed since 1993 when Kline's book was published, as have the roles and opportunities for women, but can something so engrained be changed and should it be? Today we are told that leaders must 'engage with people' which suggests that how women lead suits today's world.

The first pattern that jumps out from the interviews with women leaders was to do with their early childhood role models and its significant impact on them. This was unexpected and exciting as evidence of early childhood and its impact on who we become as a leader.

In the interviews with women leaders, two-thirds said their father was their earliest leadership role model. These positive affirmations from father to daughter seemed to give these women a significant start in building themselves as leaders. Another pattern that emerged was that those who said their mother was their role model tended to go into the public sector, while those who said their father was their role model tended to go into large corporate organizations. But it wasn't just who they chose but the comments that went with this choice that was so enlightening in how leadership starts to construct. Comments such as the feedback the women received as young girls:

- 'You can do anything in life.'

- 'My father believed women were equal.'

- 'My father treated us no different than boys'

- 'I learned values and hard work from my father.'

- 'He wanted me to succeed in everything I did but without pressure.'

- 'You can do anything you want to do.'

Hearing this positive affirmation from father to daughter had a powerful impact on these women in starting to construct their leadership. Mothers also gave positive affirmation including:

- 'Never put a label on anyone, have horizons as far and as wide as you want.'

The positive feedback continued for many of the women leaders in school. The individual teacher or head teacher was also important in helping to construct these future leaders. The majority of the women enjoyed school mainly because a certain teacher saw something in them and gave them positive affirmation. This included:

- 'He saw I had a brain and made me believe I could do things': the outcome was to become one of the top female polar explorers and now lead scientist expeditions to study climate change.

- 'Your daughter is bright and could go to university. She has a right to be there': the outcome was not only university (which was unusual for a child on a council, estate in Liverpool), but to become a chief executive in the public sector.

- 'She told my parents I was gifted and I knew she believed in me': she ended up with a PhD from Cambridge and is now director of the UK Space Agency.

These early powerful affirmations from parents and teachers are the building blocks of constructing leadership showing that fathers, mothers and teachers have a very important role to play in developing leaders. These affirmations are part of something called leadership self-efficacy.

Self-efficacy

Self-efficacy is a key construct derived from Albert Bandura's social-cognitive theory (*Social Foundation of Thought & Action: A Social Cognitive Theory*, 1986) and plays a crucial role in linking ability with

23

performance. Self-efficacy is defined as 'beliefs in one's capabilities to organize and execute the courses of action required to produce given attainments' (Bandura, 1997, p3) The belief in one's ability to perform leadership has a powerful influence on performance. According to Bandura: 'people process, weigh and integrate diverse sources of information concerning their capability, and they regulate their choice behaviour and effort expenditure accordingly' (p212).

Substantial literature shows that feelings about self-efficacy influence what people choose to do, their persistence in the face of difficulties, and how much effort they exert (Bandura, 1982; Bandura & Cervane, 1983; Bandura & Wood, 1989). Efficacy beliefs have also been shown to influence thought patterns such as whether a person is optimistic or pessimistic, as well as stress reactions. (Bandura, 1986). Self-efficacy is domain led: ie, having confidence in one's ability to lead.

It also seems that when a woman sees herself as a leader, she is motivated to lead and her engagement with leadership is to seek out more leadership responsibilities and consciously look for opportunities to develop her leadership. In other words, she is constructing leadership self-efficacy. Efficacy comes from four kinds of experiences:

- Personal performance and accomplishments.

- Role models.

- Performance feedback from credible people such as positive affirmation.

- Physiological condition and mood state: the better one feels physically and emotionally, the more confident a person feels.

Self-beliefs develop over time through life and work events when you encounter these four experiences. What the majority of the women leaders had in early childhood was positive feedback from a parent or a teacher that enabled them to start their leadership construct. In addition, the more leadership experiences a person has, the higher will be their leadership self-efficacy. However, there is a blip in this. Crystal Hoyt, University of Richmond, was exploring gender and self-efficacy for her PhD in 2002 and explored the relationship between stereotype threat, leadership efficacy and various leadership outcomes for women leaders.

The findings showed stereotype activation had the opposite effects on confident and non-confident women's perceived performance and anxiety. For highly confident women, the stereotype served to increase both their perception of their leadership performance, identification with being a leader and decrease their anxiety before leading a group. In contrast, the less confident women perceived that they performed poorly as leaders, identified less with the label of leader and were more anxious before leading a group, after being presented with the negative stereotype. Therefore confidence is important.

Additionally, Murphy, Faller, Boyd & Hogue (2001) found that when threatened, female leaders high in leadership self-efficacy were more comfortable in the leadership situation than those lower in leadership self-efficacy. The results suggest that stereotype activation serves to challenge highly efficacious women and threaten less confident women. So why are some women more confident than others when faced with leadership? It is how they interpret success. Men tend to interpret their leadership performance in a more efficacy-enhancing manner, while some women tend to attribute their successful leadership in a way that constrains efficacy growth, for example, saying the success was down to luck. This becomes a pattern that has to be addressed. This is known as 'imposter syndrome' and while it affects both women and men, it seems to be more common in women.

Imposter syndrome

Michelle Obama recently said on her UK visit:

> I still have a little imposter syndrome. It never goes away that you are actually listening to me. It doesn't go away that feeling that you shouldn't take me that seriously. What do I know? I share with you because we all have doubts in our abilities, about our power and what that power is.

We all have an 'inner critic' that is supposed to keep us out of trouble and grounded but sometimes, that critic is over-developed and becomes a voice in our heads that says, 'you are not good enough to be a leader' or 'you don't deserve the promotion'. The voice becomes loud in fear of being 'found out' and maybe you are not as good as you should be. No-one wants to feel like this but it happens to many people at least once in their working life. It is particularly high when children have over-critical parents and no positive affirmations. However, it can be turned around when women start to own and acknowledge their successes in and outside the workplace. Confidence and belief in ourselves is such an important part of leadership and vital in the development of leadership self-efficacy and successful outcomes.

Confidence

In our research with young people the biggest barrier to being a leader was lack of confidence from both girls and boys. We also found this lack of confidence far greater in the UK than other countries and found that schools in other countries integrated activities that actually built the confidence of young people. Confidence can be acquired which means this lack of confidence can be turned around.

Today this lack of confidence is affecting the millennials just as much as others with around a third suffering from imposter syndrome. Research from a career development agency found 12 million between the ages of 18 and 34 suffer from 'confidence gremlins': 52 percent feared being 'put on the spot'; two in five feared having to do a presentation; while 40 percent of women and 22 percent of males felt intimidated by senior people. In the US, Sheryl Sandberg found that millennial women were less likely than their male peers to characterise themselves as 'leaders', 'visionaries' and 'self-confident'. Therefore, this issue has to be addressed if we are to see more women leaders. Success, it turns out, correlates with confidence as much as it does with capability.

The difference between young women and men is that while both may feel doubt, it doesn't stop young men. But there is a problem with this as well. Men tend to overplay their confidence and consciously try to hide it. Someone who has studied overconfidence is Cameron Anderson, a psychologist at the University of California. In tests on students he found that men believe they are the best and in doing so display this confidence through verbal and non-verbal behaviour such as expansive body language, a low voice and speaking early at a meeting and in a calm manner. In other words they do things that make them appear confident.

This confidence also made them popular with the rest of the group. However, in time their overconfidence came across as narcissistic and people can usually spot fake confidence. The difference with truly confident people is that they don't alienate others. They believe they are good at what they do and that self-belief comes across without arrogance or narcissism. The important message for women is that being good at your job isn't enough, having confidence and belief in yourself is just as important.

Another lesson in confidence is how we respond to things. It's been found that when a course such as an advanced degree in mathematics gets hard, male students react differently to female students. Men will say, 'this is a tough course', thus placing the challenge as external. Women tend to respond, 'I knew I wasn't good enough to do this', placing the challenge as internal and blaming themselves. Why is this? With the ability to use MRI scans, it has been found that women tend to activate the amygdalae (emotional brain) more easily in response to negative stimuli than men, resulting in building stronger emotional memories of negative events or challenges. At the same time the small part of the brain that weighs up options and some call the worry centre is larger in women. However, there are ways to counteract patterns that deter us from being our best.

It has been found that risk-taking, failure and perseverance are essential to building confidence and leadership and the way boys play actually helps this. If you watch boys in the playground from the age of five, they tease one another, get rough with one another and play fight and call each other names, according to Professor Carol Dweck at Stanford University. This makes then more resilient and they don't take tough remarks personally. In the same way, sports enables boys to enjoy the wins and shake off the losses. In my study on youth it was found that girls were expected to look after siblings rather than do sports. But girls who do sports are more likely to go to university and work in male-dominated industries and earn more. In school, girls are praised for studying hard and pleasing their teachers while getting good results will enable them to go to university.

When they start work, they find that working hard is not enough and that success includes being confident. However, because the norm has been for women to be quiet when they do speak up at meetings, they are regarded as too self-opinionated. This is something men don't experience. Without resilience to discard this, a woman may keep quiet for fear of being disliked or labelled a troublemaker. Research showed that if a female chief executive talks more than everyone else, both men and women regard her as having less capability and less suited than a male chief executive who spoke the same amount. However, when a female chief executive talks less her perceived competence rose. So as women we need to be aware when we are in leadership roles to communicate succinctly and to the point.

There are those who also believe that because women have to operate within a double bind – be both male and female – it means they cannot appear confident in the same way men do. They are in fact expected to appear both confident and modest.

The final point here is that confidence is not just about feeling good about yourself. Confidence makes things happen. It turns thoughts into actions. It enables us to make good decisions and judgements. In other words it is part of leadership. As such it includes hard work and even failure, but it enables success in our careers.

Finally, Zachary Estes, a professor of marketing and psychology in Italy and previously at Warwick University, has done some research on confidence between men and women. He gave some spatial puzzles to students and found the women did worse than the men. On analysing the data he found that the reason the women had done worse was because they hadn't even attempted to answer many of the questions. He repeated the experiment telling the students that they all had to

28

at least try and solve the puzzles. This time the women scored much higher, in fact, matching the men's score.

When women do not have confidence they hesitate and hold themselves back. In other words, the outcome of low confidence is inaction. When women don't act they hold themselves back. Yet ability is equal. This relationship between confidence and action is fundamental for women leaders. Estes did a third test this time asking the students to answer each question but also report how confident they were in their answer. The women's scores dropped while the men's scores rose significantly. In other words, just by questioning women how sure they were had an adverse effect. His final test was to boost the confidence of some by telling a random group that they had done really well on the previous test. This group of both men and women improved their score dramatically showing that confidence is both fragile and self-perpetuating and how powerful positive affirmations can be.

What all this means is that ability is not the issue between men and women, but the choice the women make to not even try because of their lack of confidence. Therefore, for more women to become leaders they have to stop doubting themselves and act. It is as Sheryl Sandberg says: 'What would you do if you weren't afraid?' That is a brilliant question and worth asking yourself.

The antecedents of leadership

The women interviewed for this book had their moments of doubt, disappointment and failure, but it didn't stop them. By acting and not allowing confidence to stop us taking action we can change our thinking and behaviours because we literally change our brains.

What about those who did not have positive feedback from home or school? Or didn't enjoy school? This is another fascinating finding from the interviews. There was one who missed some of her schooling because she had to look after her mother. She founded a company that has changed the lives of many. Her work has connected her to people such as Richard Branson and now she advises governments. Another had to deal with racism at school in Glasgow making school life intolerable. Her father told her how important education was, so she carried on. Today she has a PhD and a global business. These women went on to become amazing entrepreneurs. They had to find their own way to construct their leadership and dug deep inside to do so.

Leadership isn't something you suddenly acquire on a course or because you have become a manager. It begins in childhood and is influenced by parents, teachers, out-of-school activities, friends and family. For women, the influence of fathers and male teachers is really important and shows how men must be part of building a gender-equal society. These early antecedents of leadership are best understood by the women leaders who describe their early childhood and how their leadership began. I asked each woman who was their early-life and leadership role model followed with the question: who were their leadership role models in school?

Ann Compton, senior partner, law firm

'I would say that my father had the most influence on me in my early years. He had a hard-working ethic but also provided a stable and consistent family life. I always knew where I stood with him and he displayed immense patience with me. He wanted me to succeed in everything I did, but resisted the temptation to apply additional pressure upon me. I was brought up without any notion of whether it was "appropriate" for a woman to do certain things. I then had a junior school teacher who encouraged more freedom of expression than might have been normal for his time and this encouraged me to speak out on issues which I felt were of concern.'

Shelia Richards, former general manager, Nuffield Hospital

'In my early life, my role model would have been my dad, although I would not have recognized that at the time. He was a loyal dad and everything revolved around my sister and me. Dad focused us on learning and homework. He wanted us to be hard working, successful academically and independent.'

'At school, my memory of leadership was my secondary-school rector, a burly Welshman, and my Latin teacher, a robust Scottish woman, who was married to a minister. I would have done anything to impress her with my learning and I actually achieved 100 percent in one of the Latin exams. The rector was strict and dealt with issues. He was also keen on sport and debating. I was proud to have been one of his students.'

Dara Deering, executive director, KBC Bank Ireland

'My dad was my early role model. He had a strong work ethic and I admired how he involved himself with the family. He gave me values about people and that nothing comes easily. A number of teachers were role models especially in late primary around the age of ten. In secondary school, they noticed that I was good with numbers and so encouraged me to do extra work in maths.'

Camilla Stowell, managing director, Coutts International

'My dad, who was a successful businessman, was my role model. I also looked up to sport idols such as Steve Cram and Daley Thompson. At school, it was my house mistress and her husband who was an economics teacher. I was head girl in the final year.'

Anne Jessopp, chief executive, Royal Mint

'My father was in business and worked hard. He used to say: "you can do anything you want to do". At school, there were a couple of teachers, in particular, a woman who taught economics at A level.'

Sue Gray, air vice-marshal, RAF

'My father would say, "you can do anything you want in life". He believed if you applied yourself you could do it. At school, I was the only girl doing double maths. My physics teacher and maths teacher, who were female, were good role models. I also learned a lot from another pupil – he was very clever. There was a bit of kudos being the only girl in double maths and I knew I didn't want a 9-to-5 job.'

Emma Hall is a chartered financial planner and a fellow at the Personal Finance Authority

'My dad was my role model as he worked hard and taught me my work ethic. My mum was a fantastic mother.'

Jane Hutt AM, deputy minister in the first minister's office and chief whip at the Welsh Assembly

'My parents and grandparents were my early role models. My father was a doctor and my grandfather was a Welsh socialist vicar. My father wanted to go to Africa so we all went to Uganda. I went to a government school in Kenya for girls and had some inspiring teachers. At first, we were all white but then it became mixed. Many of the black girls became leaders and influenced my life. This experience embedded in me a hatred of racism.'

Fiona Clark, head of English, Rashid School for Boys

'My father treated us girls no differently than boys. There were no pink or blue jobs, just jobs. So I put the snow chains on the tyres when we were driving on one occasion. I loved the challenge of school, particularly history, where I had a teacher who believed in me.'

Cheryl Haswell, matron, Dilke and Lydney Hospitals

'I loved primary school and my mum – she was the leader and hard working. At school, I was into sport and music, so in secondary school I was part of a brass band, the brownies then girl guides and St John's Ambulance.'

Jo Miller, chief executive, Doncaster Council

'My mum was my role model. She brought up three children on her own. We lived on a council estate in Liverpool but she always said "never put a label on anyone". She also used to say, "have horizons as far and as wide as you want". There was always a sense of possibility. The belief to be the best of yourself was instilled in me and is still with me today.

'At school, there was a primary teacher called Safford Evans from Wales. He spoke to mum when I was nine and told her "your daughter is bright and could go to university". This was a different world to us, so he took my mum to a university and showed her around. He told her "your daughter has a right to be here". He went beyond his job.'

Sacha Romanovitch, former chief executive, Grant Thornton, global accountancy firm

'My mum and great aunt Monica were my role models. I was adopted into this family of strong women. My mum never treated us as children, but adults taking us to art galleries and such. My mum's maternal aunt was very smart and astute and gave us unconditional love.

'In junior school there were two teachers who were pretty formidable but encouraged us. In secondary, the headmistress, Miss Weadon, would review every child's exam paper and she pulled me up on my handwriting and made me write properly. People today remark on my handwriting. There was also a chemistry teacher who told me to apply to Oxford which I did. Then we had a new head who said: "imagine yourself doing something and you are half way there".'

Ann Daniels, polar explorer and leader of expeditions

'I aspired to my older brothers, then, at my secondary school, my maths teacher saw I had a brain and made me believe I could do things. The result was to pass nine GCSEs.'

Paula Martin, chief executive, Cornwall Air Ambulance Trust

'My parents, and my dad in particular, were my role models. I was an only child. Dad was a successful accountant and hard working. I watched him build relationships with clients and bank managers. He was a person of good values and built his business on recognition and great integrity. He even had one of the pop group UB40 as a client. He spent time helping others and dreamt that I would follow him, but I dreamt of being a hairdresser or beauty therapist. In fact, I started selling beauty in Boots, then did a course in accounts at night school and dad taught me too.'

Rebecca Evernden, director, UK Space Agency

'My role model was a brownie leader who encouraged girls to believe they were the best. I was at a girls' grammar with a house system and I was in Sharman named after Helen. I was focused and enjoyed music. I saw Evelyn Glenny who was engaging and successful even though deaf.'

Sara Thornton, former chief constable of Thames Valley Police, now chair of the national police chiefs' council

'My parents, in particular my mother, were who I looked up to. She believed you should work hard and do your best. She was structured and active and I have inherited that. She would say, "don't complain, there are many worse off than you". My father was a clergyman so we lived next to the church. There was always a sense of people, coming in and out of the house, so I learned to be social, people focused and aware of people from all walks of life. We would have poor homeless people asking for money and instead getting a cup of tea. I became aware of a sense of service and helpfulness.

'The local school wasn't great but they made a fuss of me and the head teacher gave me personal reading lessons. In senior school, there were one or two teachers who encouraged me. I enjoyed Latin and History because the teachers were good. I was fond of ideas and debates.'

Jeanette Forbes, chief executive, PLC Group

'My grandparents, in particular my grandfather and his work ethic, is what I had as a role model. They ran their own business in the fish distribution market with my grandmother doing the books. I did end up as head girl, but was probably given that to stop me from getting into trouble which I was doing all the time. One day we were asked to work in pairs and say what we thought the other person would do with their careers. The girl I was paired up with said: "I think Jeanette will run BT one day". I will never forget that.'

Diane Savory, former chief operating officer, Superdry and now chair at GFirst

'I believe I was born an entrepreneur – with belief in myself. I didn't have inspirational parents. I found myself. I didn't enjoy school and was told to leave at 16 because I was interested in the arts not the sciences, even with eight GCSEs. I did have my parents' support.'

Dr Rabinder Buttar, chief executive and chair, Clintec International

'I was born in India and came to Scotland when I was five years old. My father was a role model. I was the eldest of five children and he wanted all of us to be educated. School was a horrible experience. It was a time of the National Front and the school wasn't great as students left at 16. There were some good teachers but I didn't feel the school environment was good for me in the centre of Glasgow. However, my parents told me education was important so I stayed after 16. The post-16 experience was difficult as an Asian, but I had a younger brother who protected me. I also had a friend that I still keep in touch with and the Scottish neighbours were nice.'

Fiona Driscoll, former chief executive of global companies, now a non-executive director at UK Research & Innovation and the Nuffield Trust

'My role model was my father, who was a clever, thoughtful, kind man. I enjoyed discussions and respected what he said. He was generous with his time. At school, the role model was the headmistress at my private day girls' school. Miss Cameron was a tiny powerhouse. She had great ambition for "my girls" and assured us that we could go on and do things. I enjoyed school.'

Donna Baddeley, chief executive, Valleys to Coast Housing

'My parents were my role models. My mother stayed at home but she was strong and resilient. Father was West Indian. They all faced prejudice including my Irish grandparents. I went to a convent school. The Headmistress was a strong role model. I was head girl at 16.'

Kully Thiarai, director, National Theatre Wales

'My parents came from the Punjab and both were illiterate. I had to look after younger siblings. Their goal for me was to have a good marriage. At secondary school there was an English teacher who encouraged me to write and explore poetry.'

Jackie Royall, managing director, Viscose Closures

'Possibly my father was my role model, but some of that was wanting to be in control of my life which I think was moving away from my mother as a role model. She didn't have a career or any control over her life. At school nothing stands out. Some rebelling against those that said I couldn't achieve. I didn't enjoy school very much.'

Linda Green, chief executive, Linda's Inns

'My father was my role model who was a successful businessman. I also saw Margaret Thatcher as a role model. I enjoyed school and sport and ended up as head girl.'

Lisa Marie Brown, managing director, Pinkinspiration

'My role model was my father who worked in construction. But then it was a challenging time when my parents divorced that affected school. I ended up helping mum at home more.'

Katherine Bennett OBE, senior vice-president, Airbus

'Both my parents were role models and an older second cousin. I went to a girls' school where I loved English and Music. The English teacher looked at things in certain ways I could connect with. My music teacher was a soprano singer and introduced me to choral singing. As a child I did a lot of observing and was described as shy and diffident.'

Jenny Tooth OBE, chief executive, UK Business Angels Association

'My grandmother was my role model – she was feisty and a feminist. I went to a girls' school where there was a wonderful headmistress – a Jean Brodie type. She believed girls should feel confident in the world, her girls were special and treated us as grown-ups. This helped me develop myself and identity.'

Tanni Grey Thompson, Paralympian,
now baroness in House of Lords

'Both parents were my role models, particularly my father. He was a feminist and believed women were equal. I was able to walk when I started school so was able to go to a mainstream school but by six I was in a wheelchair. However, I never missed a single day's school.

By seven, my spine had collapsed. My parents were told I would do this or that and so on – but my parents never saw me as different.'

Nicola Henderson, youngest ever skipper,
Clipper Round the World Race

'My mum was my role model, who was a nurse and then became involved in politics and an MP when I was eleven.'

These early-life leadership role models and positive affirmations are crucial in how we construct our leadership. The women here had varied backgrounds but early childhood was important in shaping them. What all the women had to do was find their leadership identity and this is something that seems to happen over time and part of the leadership journey.

3.

IDENTITY

'Identity development is a constructive development theory that focuses on the growth of how people construct meaning from their life experiences.'

Robert Kegan, *The Evolving Self,* 1982

How people become leaders and how they take up the leader role are fundamentally questions about identity according to many researchers (De Rue & Ashford, 2010; Ibarra et al, 2010; Lord & Hall, 2005). In my research over three years with young people and published in *Creating Leaders in the Classroom* (2007), I also found leader identity a crucial part of developing leaders especially with girls. A leader identity is not a formal position or role in an organization but actually evolves as one engages in two interrelated actions: internalising a leader identity (De Rue & Ashford, 2010) and developing a high sense of purpose (Quinn, 2004) that looks out into the world not just inward which is akin to a manager. Internalising a leader identity entails certain relational and social processes. In doing so, you come to see yourself as a leader and are seen by others as a leader (De Rue & Ashford 2010). This is fundamental in developing women leaders. Therefore, leadership is more than just an individual's self-concept.

Scott De Rue and Susan Ashford in their article, *Who Will Lead and Who Will Follow,* for the Academy of Management in October 2010 suggest three elements for constructing a leadership identity:

- The first is at an individual level whereby leadership identity is within one's own self-concept.

- The second is at a relational level that requires a woman to be seen as a leader in relationships with others such as followers or peers. This strengthens her leader identity.

- The last element De Rue and Ashford call the collective level. This is when a woman is collectively endorsed as the leader by the group, board, political party or organization. Given this strength and acknowledgement to lead, a woman's leader identity is further reinforced and becomes more stable.

What I have tried to show is that constructing a leader identity is first influenced in childhood and then it's up to us as individuals to dig deep inside to either build on that or rebuild ourselves. This construction continues in our working lives and it is our choices and actions, particularly our actions that matter. A vital part of De Rue and Ashford's model is that identity work includes a process they call 'claiming' and 'granting'. Women 'claim' leadership identity when they take actions to assert their identity, such as taking on an important project, chairing a committee, taking a promotion or taking on a leadership role outside work in the community.

'Granting' is different and involves supporting someone who wants to start a group, network or committee. This can be inside work or outside. The point here is that it is not enough to just claim if others are not granting you leadership. Leader identity can shift up and down, so you can both lose it and gain it. A woman's leader identity will strengthen enormously when others 'grant' her the leadership role and acknowledge them as leader so opportunities for this are important. By supporting someone else, you can be noticed and asked to take the leader role and so granted leader identity.

There has been recent interest in identity and greater understanding of its relevance to leadership. There seem to be two strands of theories on identity according to Roseneil & Seymoor (1999-4): a social strand and a post-structural strand. Each is different in explaining identity. The social theory strand offers a historical narrative of the development of identity conceptualised as self-identity, as the individual's conscious sense of self (Giddens, 1991). It attempts to anchor our sense of self in our maelstrom of social life, enabling individuals to construct for themselves their biographical narratives. In Giddens' terms, the self becomes a reflexive project: 'we are not what we were but what we make of ourselves'. If you study any leader at any age you will find this process. It was certainly apparent in the women leaders interviewed here.

The post-structural strand, in contrast, offers insight into the problem of identity categories, notable in the power of the construction of identity through differences. Post-structural approaches recognise the significance of context and the role and power of language and discourse in shaping organizations and social practices. Delbridge & Ezzamel (2005) state:

> The constructive role of language is perhaps the defining characteristic that distinguishes post-structural literature from other intellectual approaches ... where attention shifts decidedly towards an appreciation of the power of language in constituting the world, in the sense that language/discourse is taken as the means by which human actors engage, make sense of and construct the world.

Here we can include culture which is embedded by its everyday language. When you join certain business sectors or government departments, the first thing a person has to do is undertake to learn the language people use including acronyms. In other words, developing identity is both individual and organizational. It becomes so ingrained that people assume everyone understands these acronyms. This is particularly true in education, the police, law and health.

Identity also has a negative side. Identifying oneself as a leader is not just taking charge or focusing on using leadership for self-interest. When leaders become overly focused on being seen in a certain way in order to advance their careers, they become excessively concerned with meeting others' expectations, keep within a safe zone and disconnected from their values (Quinn, 2004). In search of recognition and approval, they can lose sight of a larger purpose. Over time, they become less and less authentic and this is a real danger as they are more likely to be engulfed by hubris.

When this occurs the strengths of the leader become their weaknesses: confidence changes to arrogance; purpose becomes obsession; and perseverance becomes dogma and intransigence. The heroic leader can start to overestimate their abilities and popularity; they discourage questions and may ridicule anyone who challenges them. An example was Margaret Thatcher. They stop listening to others and believe only they are right. This behaviour is not leadership as these individuals won't take responsibility or listen; they replace people who criticise them and regard themselves as above the law. The impact on those around them becomes apparent. When people perceive leaders as self-interested, they trust them less and feel less committed to them and their organization.

This is why a central part of constructing a leader identity and of being seen as a leader is developing an elevated sense of purpose and conveying that sense to others. Purpose challenges leaders to move outside their safe zone and shift from what is to what is possible, while facing fears to take action in spite of them. Here we can include Winston Churchill, Nelson Mandela, Gro Harlem, who was Norway's first woman prime minister, and businesswoman Anita Roddick.

The true meaning of leader comes from an ancient English word meaning path or courageous journey. The women leaders interviewed here certainly had courage, were authentic and aware that leadership identity came to them over time and was never a given.

When asked if leadership was part of their identity only one said no and said she believed her identity was that of a social change maker. When asked if they were comfortable with leader identity they all said yes with a few stating: 'I've grown into it'. This shows the dynamic role of constructing leader identity. Yet this construct does not happen for many. Why?

Leader identity is shaped by culture and beliefs about what it means to be a leader. This is why the messages of parent and teachers are so important because so often language from the media, in particular, and the language we use every day can limit those beliefs. In my study with children, by age eleven, 48 percent of boys thought they could be a leader, while only 18 percent of girls did. Gender stereotypes and roles kick in early and shape us if they are the only messages we hear. There is such an important role here for men and in particular for fathers in building an inclusive society. The women in this study made it clear that their father telling them they could do anything or be anything they wanted in life made a huge difference. It seemed to block out stereotyping to enable them to see open doors.

In most cultures, the meaning of leader is masculine and therefore the prototype is strong, decisive, assertive and independent (Bailyn, 2006; Dennis & Kunkel, 2004; Epitropaki & Martin, 2004; Willemson 2002). By contrast, women describe themselves as caring, friendly and thinking of others, so to date have tended to be regarded as lacking leadership. That is changing but not fast enough. We now realize that women are also strong, courageous and decisive. But women lack enough role models and this is fundamental to our learning as humans. In addition, empirical research shows us that women express their leadership differently. If this is so, how different would the world be today if it was normal to have 50 percent of leaders who are women in all walks of life?

To reach this pivotal point, women need to construct leader identities in spite of the subtle barriers that organizations erect that impact on women's advancement. This is a challenge and why early childhood messages, such as 'you can go as far as you want', are so important. It isn't enough to send women on courses if the context and culture of the workplace doesn't support them. Constructing leader identity includes taking on challenges at work and gaining positive feedback. This positive affirmation enables a person to step outside their comfort zone and try more leadership challenges. By doing this an individual is not only building leader identity but realizing the essence of leadership, which is to know oneself. This self-awareness should also be matched with an abundance of curiosity to learn. This was paramount to every one of the woman leaders interviewed here.

The desire and excitement of learning throughout a life keeps leaders in touch with everything and everyone around them.

Learning

'Leadership and learning are indispensable to each other.'

From the speech JF Kennedy prepared for Dallas, Texas before he was shot in November 1963

Learning is far more than acquiring skills or regurgitating knowledge. It requires what Jean Piaget called 'learning through accommodation'. This is a learning process that allows us to change existing ideas in order to take in new information and understanding. It means altering an existing belief or idea as a result of new experiences. One of the women said: 'I used to believe leadership was all about power but later realised that in fact leadership is far more complex'.

Learning through accommodation occurs throughout life when experiences introduce new information that conflicts with existing schemas or beliefs of our world. An individual must then accommodate this new learning to ensure that what's inside their head conforms to what we see outside in the world. We also need to acknowledge that learning and constructing leadership includes emotions.

The emotional attachment of learning experiences is important. One of the leaders said that while no tutors stood out at university, 'the whole experience of going to Cambridge felt it was a privilege and opportunity'. She added: 'I grafted really hard and was immensely proud of my first-class degree'. All the women here continued to learn in constructing their leadership using different 'multiple intelligences' including logic, creativity and naturalistic learning, depending on the context in which they found themselves. Therefore learning wasn't just studying and reading, but always learning from others and using touch, feel and doing.

In addition, observing others, whether holding meetings or dealing with challenges, was common. They also used others as informal mentors, took on challenges that were new to both themselves and the organization, showing they could deal with risk. This ability to take on the challenge of constructing leadership was possible because of those who made them believe in themselves as children including parents and teacher.

In my own research with young people the most common reason for not regarding themselves as a leader was 'I'm not good enough', yet when we enabled every young person in the school to practice leadership this perception started to change. Practice and experience seem to be a base to begin in developing leadership yet most people never even try because of the beliefs and thinking that has been developed in their youth. This becomes a barrier to learning.

After around 60 years of leadership courses in universities and organizations, we look at our world and see huge failures in leadership. This is a challenge that some academics themselves have commented on such as Schon (1967, p8): 'what aspiring practitioners need most to learn, professional schools seem least able to teach.'

Professor Warren Bennis wrote on his blog: 'universities operate too much like a guild system, throwing out students with dissertations without practical knowledge'. Whereas the past dean of Harvard Business School, Professor Nitin Nohria said: 'to make more progress in the education of leaders, we have to get better at translating knowing into doing'.

Professor Keith Grint at Warwick University examined these shortcomings further by exploring the distinctions originally identified by Aristotle and the ancient Greeks that still apply to us today. In his sixth book, *Nicomachean Ethics*, Aristotle identifies two main types of knowledge or intellect: *sophia* and *phronesis*. *Sophia*, he explains, involves reasoning and universal truths. *Phronesis* involves rational thinking too, but also considers action that will bring desired outcomes or effects. Aristotle argued that *phronesis* is not simply a skill (*techne*) that involves the ability to decide how to achieve a certain end, but also the ability to reflect upon and determine good end results that are consistent with the aim of 'living well'.

While Aristotle argues that *sophia* is a more serious pursuit, he says the highest pursuit of knowledge and good in the world requires both, because *phronesis* facilitates *sophia*. With *phronesis*, or practical wisdom, intelligence is required and soundness of judgement in practical contexts is needed.

Many of the women interviewed talked about how their experiences were their greatest learning tool. Grint concludes that it is only by doing leadership that we can gain the wisdom of leaders and that this implies the rethinking of educating leaders. He proposes that knowledge can be taught in lectures, skills through practice and wisdom comes from experiencing leadership itself. The women leaders were proficient in all three. However, they said they also learned from other people, books, talks and everyday life or just being in the world. Every one of these women was curious and wanting to continually learn. A few of the women went on to study a master's degree after five years. Learning enabled them to be effective and deal with some difficult challenges.

There is something else that also impacts on constructing leadership that is triggered in early childhood and included in the antecedents of leadership. It is vital for any leader to develop good, healthy interpersonal skills. This does not mean that as a leader you have to be charismatic or totally outgoing. In fact, many of the best leaders are introverts, but when they do speak they are listened to. In any leadership situation, individuals need to connect and communicate with others. This is something the scientist Alan Turing had to realise when working on how to break German codes during World War II as shown in the film, *The Imitation Game*, starring Benedict Cumberbatch.

The quest to understand and practice leadership is not an isolated process but rather a journey of transformation and growth. The power of this transformative growth is akin to the alchemy of old with its blend of philosophy, science, art, spirituality and psychology. The primary purpose of the alchemists wasn't to change lead into gold, but to transform the ordinary into the exalted or, as some would say, to transform leaden consciousness to golden consciousness. Gold signified the ability to manifest a spiritual truth on the physical world.

A true leader is an inner alchemist who is able to transmute base emotions and thoughts into more developed ones, to learn new behaviour patterns, and to turn primitive behaviour patterns into more sophisticated and adequate ones for today's world. Leadership is not something you just learn on a course but is something each one of us must construct as part of ourselves. In doing so we develop what is known as leadership identity. It enables individuals to know who they are as a leader and for others to recognise them as a leader. Learning is the journey.

Early career support

In their early careers most of the women leaders did not have a plan but were building on what they could learn from others around them. This is how they described those early years in their careers. I asked them if anyone encouraged and supported them in their early careers, as well as provide leadership role models.

Ann Compton, senior partner, law firm

'There were a couple of women partners at the firm I did my training contract at. They were relatively young and dynamic and I think were probably my first influencers in the work environment. They were also quite different in terms of temperament and I learned that it is possible to fit into a role, with all the expectations around that, and still be myself.

'When I first came to work in a large firm at one year qualified the managing partner was a man called Tim. He was hugely influential upon the firm and all who worked with him. Again, he was quite a character and I was encouraged by him to take on responsibility and to be myself. He trusted me with some significant clients and jobs. He was also able to lift you up with just a few words. He was one of those people who you always wanted to stop and speak with because he could make you feel so good about yourself and the work you were doing. Conversely if he had something more negative to feedback to you, you could be sure you would hear it straight. He had drive, energy and ambition for the firm and was way ahead in his strategic thinking of how a law firm should be run. I learned many lessons from him. Other partners also had an influence upon me for varying reasons, but Tim Barter was undoubtedly the most influential.'

Shelia Richards, former general manager, Nuffield Hospital

'I left home and went into the Scottish health service on a national management training course: two years of fantastic learning, but also a lesson on why I did not want to work in the NHS. Many staff did not have the patients at heart. It was all politics, hierarchy and no financial awareness. I have no recollection of good role models other than Barbara Young, whom I remember talking to us as an ex-trainee.

'I moved straight to London after the Scottish health service course finished to join an American healthcare company. A vision of running my own hospital and moving away from home were my drivers. The American company was male dominated but they recognized that I would work hard to achieve results and they rewarded me both financially and by giving me opportunities. I was 27 when I ran my first hospital and was the first of a few women who made that grade. I stayed with that American company for four years. Leadership to me then was hard work, hard play and I had occasion to watch how some leaders took advantage of their positions.

'Then I moved on to my second American company and started to see demonstrations of real and earned leadership. My French Canadian boss was superb – the best that I have had in my entire career. He was personable; a teacher; tough but fair; and expected that you gave the company all you had to give. The company itself had strong ethics and attracted people who were a pleasure to work with. I stayed there for seven years, the last five of which I had the chance to set up my own hospital from scratch. At that stage my French Canadian boss summed me up as an excellent administrator with a lot to learn about management and leadership.'

Camilla Stowell, managing director, Coutts International

'I've had great bosses throughout my career. Will Jones at Lloyds Bank when I spent six months in a regional office was patient and brought out the best in people. He was ambitious and stretched me. At Schroders Asset Management, Julian Windsor was my boss an ex-rifleman in the Royal Green Jackets. I added diversity and loved selling. It was an intellectual culture. Julian would let you have a go and then coach you to be better. He also made me pay attention to detail. He believed that you get back what you put in and organized a 100-mile run in the Himalayas. It was very hard but amazing.'

Anne Jessopp, chief executive, Royal Mint

'I started at Rolls-Royce in Derby but left after a year as I didn't enjoy it. "You must look like this" was the corporate message. I then went to Procter & Gamble. I had a boss who was experienced, comfortable with himself, generous with time and spirit, who gave opportunities. It developed and pushed me into different roles and, as a role model, showed that I could be different. It gave me courage to try things.'

Cheryl Haswell, matron, Dilke and Lydney Hospitals

'Donna Mead was my tutor in Wales. She was inspiring. I wanted to be a nurse officer and she understood that. I also had Jane Cumming, who is chief nurse for England today, as a mentor. Jane encouraged me to go for every opportunity. I went for a sister's post at 27.'

Emma Hall is a chartered financial planner and a fellow at the Personal Finance Authority

'I looked to strong women. I wanted to have my own money and look after myself. I had jobs from the age of 13 at weekends, as did friends. It was my goal to have a career and family.'

Jo Miller, chief executive, Doncaster Council

'Gerry Hutchinson was a good role model when I was a trainee solicitor. He allowed me to break some rules, but never to go so far as to get into trouble. Also Dame Eve Buckland who always engaged with front line staff not just the hierarchy and told me, "you can go to the next level". She was honest and said that to do so would mean to move and not to fear that.'

Sue Gray, air vice-marshal, RAF

'All my line managers have been supportive. I enjoyed working on the VC-10 and took over from another female which was unusual. The flight sergeant was brilliant as was my immediate boss.'

Fiona Clark, head of English, Rashid School for Boys

'I worked with the National Trust after doing a secretarial course following university and became a "floater" moving around the organization which was a great way to see and understand every part. I loved the media work where there were two brilliant press officers, Nicola Drysdale and Caroline Harrison. The two of them were inspiring and thorough in their work so I enjoyed working with them. I left in 1995 to focus on something new rather than just an old way of doing things.'

Jane Hutt AM, chief whip at the Welsh Assembly

'I became a community worker in the Welsh valleys and then in Newport. I set up the first women's aid refuge in Cardiff and joined the Labour Party when Margaret Thatcher became prime minister.'

Sacha Romanovitch, former chief executive,
Grant Thornton, global accountancy firm

'The chemistry degree I was doing was four years with a year doing research and I had to support my grant, so I designed and made dresses, and thought I might go into design after university. Then a woman came and gave a talk from an accountancy firm and I decided that this is what I would do. So I began as an accountant working for a small firm that became part of a large well-known company.'

Ann Daniels, polar explorer and leader of expeditions

'I took a job in a bank and enjoyed this. I wanted to do banking exams so I could be more than a bank teller. I told my manager but a guy who had joined two weeks after me with just five GCSEs was given that opportunity not me. I was told he was chosen because "he's a man". I was pretty hacked off and became more determined so applied myself to work hard. I progressed slowly and was even asked to train a graduate in a job I wasn't allowed to do. I agreed to this but negotiated a promotion and then I progressed quicker. No-one inspired me. I fought all the way.'

Paula Martin, chief executive, Cornwall Air Ambulance Trust

'I ran a holiday accommodation business in Cornwall and had my daughter. As I became older I thought I should have a proper career. I was married to a farmer so agriculture became my learning. When my daughter went to university, I began to wonder what should I be.

'I worked hard on a European project for a national charity in farming, managing a team of bio-diversity specialists to encourage farmers to stop using pesticides and switch to sustainable biodiversity. I wrote the funding for three years but we ran out of funds at the end of three years so wrote for more as I felt responsible for everyone as they had bills to pay and needed certainty. Then a wonderful opportunity came my way. A programme called the Challenge of Rural Leadership organized by Plymouth University and the Worshipful Company of Farmers. I was part of 20 peers from agriculture and food production. The programme included the theory of leadership, personal effectiveness and the difference between management and leadership. It was the first time I'd done any structured learning like it and it blew my mind.'

Rebecca Evernden, director, UK Space Agency

'I worked in publishing for a while doing a postgrad. Marjorie Scardino was the chief executive, the first at a FTSE 100 company. She was very present, engaging and talked to everyone. She was a strong figurehead. Then I joined the civil service and went on the fast stream scheme. I worked at Defra where I had a line manager who encouraged me through the first couple of years supporting me and showing me what I could do. Helen Ghosh was permanent secretary. I worked on a project called climate adaptation and had a good line manager. She supported me when I worked part-time after having a baby. We moved to York and I was still working in London so it was a challenge.'

Sara Thornton, former chief constable of Thames Valley Police, now chair of the national police chiefs' council

'I was interested in the public sector then a colleague mentioned the graduate scheme with the police. I went and had a look but spent the first two years in the security service, then joined the police graduate scheme. The programme included a mentor and my second mentor was supportive over a long time. He put me in touch with key people, encouraged me to reflect and provided different perspectives that helped. There was a shift from listening to parents to listening to peers.'

Jeanette Forbes, chief executive, PLC Group

'There was no-one as a leadership role model or mentor in those early days, but I did enjoy films such as Working Girl with Melanie Griffiths and Sigourney Weaver, thinking I'd like to be successful like that.'

Diane Savory, former chief operating officer,
Superdry and now chair at GFirst

'I worked for a fashion company and had a female boss who was sassy. I used to call her my second mum. She believed in me but died young. That gave me strength to push harder.'

Dr Rabinder Buttar, chief executive and
chair, Clintec International

'I worked in London for five years before moving to Germany to work for a Japanese company. I then launched my consultancy business. My husband was a dentist so there was a regular income. We came back to Scotland and I grew my business.'

Fiona Driscoll, former chief executive of global
companies, now a non-executive director at UK
Research & Innovation and the Nuffield Trust

'I was at Deloitte where people were clever but I didn't find a leadership role model. They tended to adopt me rather than mentor me. But the partners did look after me.'

Donna Baddeley, chief executive, Valleys to Coast Housing

'I fell into housing in 1987 as a housing officer. I knew I was in the right place. I moved up quickly and took an executive post at 26. During the 1980s I gained professional qualifications in housing. In 1985 I did an MBA and then an MA in organizational development.'

Kully Thiarai, director, National Theatre Wales

'I worked with a small theatre group and artistic director Graham Devlin where I trained by working from the bottom up. This was such an amazing experience I stayed in Yorkshire. A woman took over as artistic director of the Red Ladder Touring Theatre Company based in Yorkshire. She was generous and collaborative while being clear about what she wanted. Through my work there I met everyone in that world, so I became the company stage manager. We toured into youth clubs with new plays. Being a qualified social worker, it bridged my two areas: youth outside schools and aspirations in the theatre.'

Jackie Royall, managing director, Viscose Closures

'I had a great line manager who believed in me. No coaching or anything like that in those days, but he would just tell me that he believed in me. He let me get on and would praise work in front of others. Things turned round when I won Welsh Woman of the Year. There was also a tipping point of personal development when I attended a Dale Carnegies twelve-week course. Mixing with other senior people and realising they were just people, not different to me. This gave me the confidence that I was good enough as a person. I then studied Six Sigma and did much reading, learning and developing. Writing up my dissertation and reflecting on the literature review taught me that how I thought was right and I needed to learn how to articulate what was in my head.'

Lisa Marie Brown, managing director, Pinkinspiration

'I did temp work and learned from people. After a series of jobs I went to university. When I decided to work in construction, I bought pink hard hats and high viz jackets from the US. My thoughts were "how can we upskill young people and women" so set up Pink Ladies. They were taught tiling, plastering etc. We gave awards and this hit the media. I went around Newport and high-poverty areas of South Wales to encourage women into business.'

Katherine Bennett OBE, senior vice-president, Airbus

'Early in my career I worked for an American woman in a PR company.

The woman made a real effort to show gratitude after I had worked hard and late on a project. It showed me how effort and saying well done meant to people.'

Jenny Tooth OBE, chief executive, Business Angels Association

'I worked for Egon Ronay – I was his PR assistant. I spent time in France and he taught me how to appreciate good food and wine. We visited lots of restaurants. He was inspirational.'

Tanni Grey Thompson, Paralympian,
now baroness in House of Lords

'My role models started with Kathryn Switzer, the first woman to run the Boston marathon in 1967, when a race official, Jock Semple, tried hard to push her off. It was only in 1984 that women were allowed to run a marathon as it was thought it would prevent them having children. Women were allowed to pole vault in 2000 as it had been thought this would damage the uterus and again stop them from having children. Whereas for me, they said it would kill someone in a wheelchair to do a marathon.'

Nicola Henderson, youngest ever skipper,
Clipper Round the World Race

'I took a gap year as I couldn't wait to get out of an institution and went sailing. I wanted to travel and try working abroad. I did my day-skipper exam then found a boat. For three months I sailed and was the youngest and had my teddy bear with me – I was 18. I listened and watched; cooked meals and learned. I found myself quietly stepping into leadership roles.'

Each of these women began as we all do, feeling our way in a career but what is clear is that to do more than a job women start to construct their leader identity. Learning is fundamental along with continued role models, mentors and positive affirmation. Each woman is different and has to find her own path but continuous learning is vital. It is through learning that we gain wider perspectives or the ability to see things more than one way. Gaining perspectives enables each to be a more effective leader in today's fast moving, complex world. This can come from expanding your horizons by trying different roles to travelling the world. Each contributes to building leader identity and widening perspectives.

4.

PERSPECTIVE

'The only real voyage of discovery consists not in seeing new landscapes, but in having new eyes, in seeing the universe with the eyes of another, of hundreds of others, in seeing the hundreds of universes that each of them sees.'

Marcel Proust

Learning and leadership identity aren't enough today when the world is so unpredictable, volatile, complex and ambiguous. Leaders need to be more than managers. American business author Tom Peters wrote: 'the difference between managers and leaders is the difference between day and night. The former honour stability, control through systems and procedures. Leaders thrive on change.'

What we know from research is that many managers do not want to be leaders because they have become socialised into this other paradigm called management. Right now, the world needs innovation, transformation and courage to address the challenges we are faced with. The world is crying out for leaders not managers or technocrats. As David Whyte the poet writes: 'in the future, the word manager will disappear from our understanding of leadership, and thankfully so'.

Many of the post-war generation, including management thinkers, wanted to change how we ran the world but instead management colleges such as Ashridge and Henley were set up and management was made into a profession in itself. Of these, W. Edwards Deming, who started the quality revolution in Japan, said: 'our prevailing system of management has destroyed our people. People are born with intrinsic motivation, self-esteem, dignity, curiousity to learn, joy in learning'. He saw this destruction beginning in families and schools and following a person's life. He blamed hierarchical management where power in organizations was used to disproportionately reward those at the top and separate them from others. Today we have seen the reality of this across the public sector and business. Our hierarchies will not change until we see the world differently.

The way to change the present worldview is to change our thinking. When interviewing the women leaders, it was clear that one of the key findings about their mindset was that egos were non-existent as they talked about the people who had supported and influenced them to become leaders. They were open to new ideas and consistently learning. They were not afraid to try new things and explore things from different perspectives. This chapter is going to show you how to develop multiple perspectives in constructing new thinking for leaders today. It begins with how the brain works.

Assumptions

We have billions of neurons in the brain making connections that look like a city lit up at night. They develop all our lives but usually have two stages of huge growth. The first is from birth to around two years and then again as teenagers. Both babies and teenagers need greater sleep while this is going on and it explains why teenagers don't want to get up in the morning. Each of these neurons has an assumption about the world and ourselves attached to it and together with other connections creates our own world view. This is how we see reality and no two people see reality quite the same. When two people look at a building or a piece of art they will each see it differently. The colours may be brighter for one person or they may not see that one side of the building has more windows. Each one of us creates our reality based on billions of assumptions so some people will regard the world as a dangerous place and never explore it; while others will perceive the world as an exciting place full of discovery and interesting people. As the physicist David Bohm wrote: 'what we think about reality can alter our relationship with it'.

In addition, everything we do in each moment of the day is a reflexive response. Our brain uses experience to acquire assumptions and applies these across contexts. These assumptions are so powerful they make you the person you are. Therefore, you are your assumptions, whether they are about the world or yourself. They can limit your life and stop you trying new things or they can open your life to new experiences. We now know, thanks to work of scientist Benjamin Libet in the 1980's, that the decisions we make come from the unconscious hundreds of milliseconds before they reach our conscious awareness. So our assumptions are indeed powerful.

The problem is that many assumptions are flawed or misguided including those often made about how to develop leadership. The assumption is often that the problem in organizational behaviour and poor performance is the result of deficiencies in individuals. So they send them on courses or for coaching to improve employees' skills, knowledge and attitudes. Therefore the target for improvement and change is the individual.

However, individuals do not work in isolation but within a culture, context and structure that will have an impact on them. So let's turn the assumption around. The problem with organizational behaviour and poor performance comes from a poorly designed and ineffective managed system. Changing the system to support and demand new behaviours will enable learning that will result in improving performance and effectiveness. Therefore, the primary target for change and development is the organization. That doesn't mean employees are not developed, but it begins with the organization. This is a mistake many make. These assumptions form into what is called implicit theories. Let's explore our leadership implicit theories.

Implicit theories

Here's a challenge for you from my colleague Dr Tracey Manning. Which one of these statements is the true one?

- Leadership is natural; leaders are mostly born.

- Leaders are charismatic, confident, strong and extravert.

- To be a leader, you need a leadership position/role and power.

- To become a better leader, you need to work on your leadership weaknesses.

- Organizations succeed or fail due to their leadership.

The answer is none. The statements reflect aspects of implicit leadership theories based on assumptions about how leaders look, behave and develop. These assumptions are inside the heads of people when they attend courses and are powerful enough to stay in place at the end of the programme. In other words, if I believe leaders are tall, charismatic and bossy, then I'm not a leader because my implicit theory doesn't fit with who I believe I am. In addition, these implicit theories are culturally shared, but include some assumptions held in common around the world, as was shown by the Globe project led by the late Professor Robert House from the Wharton School of Business, University of Pennsylvania.

What about the implicit views we have of ourselves and others? Answer the next three questions honestly and don't procrastinate so your answer is instinctive.

- If you had to choose, would you take (a) lots of success, rewards and pats on the back or (b) lots of challenges, including new and difficult ones?

- When do you feel smartest and pleased with yourself: (a) after an outstanding performance or (b) after you've just learned something difficult and challenging?

- Do you believe that (a) each person only has so much leadership potential to develop or (b) that leadership is an almost infinitely expandable capacity?

According to implicit theory, how we see ourselves and others falls into two categories. The first is called Entity where a person sees oneself in such a positive light that it undermines learning. Their motive is self enhancement and looking good to the world. The second category is called Incremental whereby a person's desire is to improve one's capabilities and effectiveness. The motive is self-improvement that includes reflecting on experiences. All of the women leaders interviewed fell into this latter category. The first category was brilliantly expressed by T.S. Eliot:

'Half of the harm that is done in the world
is due to people who want to feel important
...They do not mean to do harm...
They are absorbed in the endless struggle
to think well of themselves.'

T.S. Eliot, *The Cocktail Party*

Mindset

The work on implicit theories was taken up by Carol Dweck, professor of psychology at Stanford University, who expanded and simplified the concept to mindset. She described mindset as a theory that provides a mental framework that guides how people think, feel and act in challenging situations, especially when learning or when setbacks are encountered. There are two categories 'fixed' and 'growth' mindset. If you answered (a) for the questions above, they fall into the fixed mindset and if you answered (b) you have a growth mindset. However, some people have a mix of both while others are clearly one or the other depending on their beliefs.

A fixed mindset regards intelligence as static. A person with a fixed mindset will avoid challenges, give up easily and see effort as fruitless. They will also be threatened by others' success and avoid negative feedback. Their desire is to look good. We can all think of leaders and employees with a fixed mindset. In many situations, this can be changed but what sometimes happens is that an organization decides to have managers coach others and, without realising it, a small number of those managers with a fixed mindset will transfer this to the people they are coaching. You can end up with an area of the organization where a fixed mindset becomes the norm.

It is believed that those with fixed mindsets may be over-represented in management and senior positions. Yet individuals and organizations can greatly increase productivity and work satisfaction through changing fixed mindsets. Finally, a whole organization can suffer from a fixed mindset which creates what is called a 'culture of genius'. An example of a such an organization is one with a high-potential scheme for a few, especially if the aim is just to get on the scheme, as it fulfils the desire to look good which drives this mindset.

In contrast a growth mindset will regard intelligence as something that is developed throughout life. A person with a growth mindset will embrace challenges, persist when there are setbacks and regard effort as mastery. They have a strong desire to learn and are inspired by others, while regarding criticism as a learning opportunity. Key to a growth mindset is the ability to reflect and question assumptions. This opens up the mind to new ideas and thinking. A leader with a growth mindset will achieve far more and be a better boss and role model. A growth mindset will create an organization where space and resources are used for real learning. Both individuals and the organization are open to transformation.

Having a growth mindset is only the start in developing the thinking for today's complex and uncertain world. Leaders today have to go further. They have to deal with problems where they may not have the answer or the challenge is so complex that what may be thought a solution can actually create another problem. Today these are called 'wicked' problems and the work of Keith Grint at Warwick University has enabled leaders to understand this. His model describes three different types of problems and how they should be tackled. This is something all women leaders need to understand.

Problems today

The first in Grint's model he calls 'tame' problems that may be complicated but are resolvable through single linear acts that follow each other and these problems are mostly resolved by one person. Tame problems are likely to have occurred before, so are not new. Managers do this all the time. What is noticeable is that these problems have only a limited degree of uncertainty and there is always an answer. Someone calls in sick and a replacement has to be found, for example.

The second type of problem Grint calls 'critical' problems that are usually associated as a crisis. There is little time for making a decision and so a command style of leadership takes the helm and acts.

However, today we face problems that are complex, rather than complicated, are ambiguous, are unpredictable and can change at any time. These are called 'wicked' problems. They cannot be removed from their environment to be resolved. They go beyond either/or solutions and there is no clear relationship between cause and effect. The problem can go on and on with no obvious solution. These include environmental issues, which it will take more than science to solve. Leaders often fail to realise how different problems are interrelated. Poverty, growth of cities, use of chemicals and plastic, education and farming are challenges that are being resolved through national policies and global cooperation. In addition, too often leaders fail to see how their solutions affect and impact on future generations. The type of decisions often made by political leaders is called 'disjointed incrementalism' but today these are less and less effective.

In addressing wicked problems in these challenging times, the leader has the role of asking the right questions rather than providing the right answers. It also requires collective leadership as no one person can resolve the problem. Engaging the community to face up to the problem and be involved in the solution is also required. Today leaders have to deal with more of these wicked problems whether in business, politics or society on a global scale. The challenge is that organizations have developed cultures and structures whereby people and our brains like to do what we have done before, so it is easier to try and resolve these problems with management or command when in fact, leadership is required.

The leader has to accept that they do not have the answer alone and that any answer will take a long time to resolve with everyone taking responsibility. This is a challenge for any leader as people are used to hierarchy where the top is expected to know the answer and just tell everyone else what to do. This mindset often begins in families and schools and translates into the workplace. In addition, those who have reached the top by being effective managers will struggle in today's world. The challenges most quoted by managers include:

- New technologies that disrupt old work practices

- Information overload

- Interconnections of systems and communities

- Dissolving traditional organizational barriers

- Different values and expectations of the new generation entering the workplace

- Increased globalisation and leading across cultures

What stood out with the women leaders interviewed here was their ability to communicate and connect with people and use leadership rather than management to address their issues. Critical to this was their continual ability to learn. This is because understanding reduces the complexity of data and then together wicked problems are more likely to be resolved, though not overnight.

How do leaders work in this environment and why is this so important for women today? In the section under learning I mentioned Jean Piaget, a Swiss psychologist. His work differed from others in the first half of the 20th century, who were more focused on intelligence tests. Piaget believed that children thought differently to adults and went through development stages, including their ability to think, which became more sophisticated until they became adults. However, with advances in neuroscience and MRI scanners we now know that the brain doesn't stop developing as an adult but rather keeps on developing throughout life, especially if we keep learning. Robert Kegan, a Harvard professor in adult learning and professional development, has built on Piaget's work with far-reaching consequences for women leaders.

The development of the conscious mind

For Kegan, it's not skills or even information that needs developing for our complex world, but how we think. While constructing our leadership we also need to explore the construction of an individual's understanding of reality and the development of that construction to more complex levels. This is not what a person knows, but the way they know those things. This is because our brain creates what we see and gives it meaning. Think of the well-known drawing that we can see as either a beautiful woman or an old woman with a long chin. But this is either/or perception: what if we need to see more than either/or as in the case of the complex wicked problems we've just explored?

Today, we have to see things from multiple perspectives. There is a well-known story about three blind men and an elephant. The men were walking along when their sticks told them there was a large item ahead and the smell told them it was an animal of some kind. The first blind man went up and felt the elephant's tusk and said: 'this is a very hard creature'. The second blind man went up to the elephant and felt his leg saying: 'this is a very leathery creature, but also warm and soft'. The third blind man went up to the elephant and felt its tail saying: 'this is a hairy animal'. Each blind man saw something different. Leaders today have to try and see the whole elephant as well as all the parts.

According to Kegan our frameworks of how we see the world and ourselves can evolve to see more deeply and in multiple perspectives. He has developed five ways, or orders of consciousness, of constructing reality, each more sophisticated to deal with more complex problems that today's leaders have to resolve. Each order of consciousness is a qualitative shift in making meaning of our world and its understanding of the complexity. It is not hierarchical. But there is a cost if people don't move to the next order of consciousness or have the capacity to meet the demands of their organization that shows itself as stress to the individual.

The first two orders of consciousness usually occur in childhood. The first is about developing perceptions based on the reality of what a baby or small child sees. The second development or order of consciousness is when children notice others' reactions, so they think: 'I'm a friendly person, not so much because I'm happy, but because I've noticed it's true about me in lots of situations'. So the shift moves from what a child sees to how others perceive them and being aware of this.

The third development usually occurs in adolescence and Kegan calls this the socialised order. This is where we move beyond our own needs and take in the values and expectations of those around us who instinctively matter to us: parents, siblings, friends or a teacher. We become aligned to others and society, so we are able to co-ordinate data and have different points of view within our own role. We learn trust and take responsibility within a larger social structure. We can stay at this conscious level. Most adults who use this meaning-making system are quite successful. However, this level of consciousness will not solve today's challenges. It is as Albert Einstein said: 'we cannot solve our problems with the same thinking we used when we created them'.

The fourth development Kegan calls self-authoring because it enables the person to step back and form their own judgements, ideology and belief system through which they become their own person rather than dictated by society. They can co-ordinate multiple roles because they have a strong sense of their own identity. For a woman, this means she can be wife, mother, director, leader and follower without conflict. This is why I asked the women how they felt with having 'leader' as part of their identity and also how good a follower they were. Those with this consciousness have a larger perspective through which to judge, negotiate and make sense of reality. They take responsibility for their own emotions and will take a stand if necessary. Yet their response to problems tends to be to create laws and this is not enough to solve warring ideologies in the world.

The final consciousness development is called self-transformation. Here individuals can hold more than one system or perspective, in fact, embrace contradiction and paradox. They can hold multiple perspectives, moving completely away from the either/or reality. Instead they compare them, wary of any single one. People here discover what is true by logical discussion or dialogue and through considering opposite theories. This is the thinking that is required today from leaders.

Kegan says we are a species in peril and know it, for we are both creative and destructive. Who is going to resolve the complex problems we have to deal with today? Unfortunately, this fifth way of thinking seems to only occur in those over 40 years of age and in only 1 percent of the population. Therefore, this conscious development needs to be part of constructing leaders. How are we going to increase the number of these leaders? I believe by enabling many more women to express their leadership, as I found women tend to be able to hold multiple perspectives as part of my work in mentoring directors. Without being able to develop our thinking we all run the risk of remaining in Plato's cave.

Plato tells of prisoners chained to a cave since birth unable to turn their heads. All they can see is the wall of the cave. Behind them burns a fire and between the fire and the prisoners is a raised walkway where people pass daily carrying animals or wood or food. To the prisoners this is what reality looks like. For years the prisoners believe what they see on the wall is the world. One day one of the prisoners escapes and climbs out of the cave and is shocked to see the world and the sunshine. He realises that his previous beliefs about the world were wrong. He goes on an intellectual journey where he discovers beauty and meaning. He returns to the cave to tell the rest of the prisoners but they do not believe him and threaten to kill him if he tries to free them.

How does this relate to the challenges we face today? Think of the task of stopping global climate change, gang culture or radicalism. Think of the issue of gender equality. How does Plato's cave relate to these? What keeps people tied to the cave? The answer is fear and insecurity. For a leader fear and insecurity must be replaced with courage and self-determination. This can be a challenge.

Insecure attachment

Some of this fear comes from 'attachment security'. My colleague Dr Tracey Manning has done much work with attachment and leadership in the US. Let's first clarify what attachment is.

If early caregivers are responsive to children's needs, children are likely to develop 'secure attachment' to be comfortable with themselves and others, enjoying close relationships while able to be independent. If caregivers are perceived as unresponsive or inconsistently responsive to children's needs, children develop 'insecure attachment' styles, are less trusting, anxious about and avoidant of relationships, or both. Whether secure or insecure, attachment is deep and tends to stay with us into adulthood. What is also worth noting is that many of those at the top of organizations have insecure attachment as this drives them. It also results in poor interpersonal skills such as communication.

In their article 'Back to basics: Applying a Parenting Perspective to Transformational Leadership' in *The Leadership Quarterly*, Popper & Mayseless (2003) stated that adult attachment theory could provide valuable insights into leadership processes and leader-follower relations. In times of uncertainty or collective crisis research shows that individuals appear to need strong leadership. According to Popper & Mayseless, creating a sense of security is the way a leader empowers followers, increases their self-esteem, creativity, autonomy and well-being, resulting in noticeable effects on group performance and productivity. The failure of a leader to empower followers appears to be a key factor in performance and productivity. We also know from previous research that insecure attached managers are less likely to delegate responsibility and power to others but create centralised authority structures.

There are different types of insecure attachment and each has a different effect on leadership. Attachment-anxious people tend to pursue goals associated with their unfulfilled needs for love and support and their desire to be accepted. In contrast, attachment-avoidant individuals, pursue goals that fit their self-reliance and distance from others. These differences will also impact on their motivation to lead as well as how they lead. Attachment also influences how we view ourselves. Anxious-attachment individuals will view themselves less positively, whereas, avoidant-individuals exhibit little self-criticism in achievement-related areas, but not in more social or emotional areas. What impact does this have on followers?

Avoidant-attachment leaders seem to result in followers more likely to suffer from poorer mental health and wellbeing, especially those followers with anxious attachment. In other words, attachment-related leadership are not only visible in behaviour but visible by followers and affect their social and emotional mental health and wellbeing. Attachment-anxious leaders tend to focus on their own needs for approval and security revealing their lack of confidence or leadership self-efficacy.

This is why attachment security, particularly in these times is so important, as secure attachment in both leaders and followers is vital in challenging, ambiguous and unpredictable times where strong communication and interpersonal skills are crucial.

Constructing leaders is complex as we see in the insights from all the women interviewed. Each had their own journey to travel, as do each of us, but their key was to continually learn and grow as a leader.

PART 2:
CREDIBILITY

Just as constructing a leader identity is an active ongoing process, so credibility is built on with hard work. It has several elements to it, but the essence of credibility is that a person will do what they say they will do. In other words, they keep their promises and fulfil commitments but, above all, are consistent, as it is through consistency that leaders build trust. This is not about filling a tool box with management techniques but rather building character and knowing who you are and what you can achieve with others. Having aspiration and drive without credibility makes working life hard for colleagues around you.

There's an old leadership book called Leadership Jazz written by the American furniture maker Max DuPree. In it he tells the story of being with his small premature granddaughter during her first days. The nurse told them to touch and talk to the baby so she could: 'be able to connect your voice to your touch'. This too, DePree said, was fundamental for leaders in building credibility.

As a leader, you first have to find your voice. You have to know who you are – what some today call your authentic self. Why is this so important? Over the last few years leaders from business, banking, charities and politics have lost public trust. At the same time leaders have to deal with geopolitics, regulators, a digital world, natural disasters, social media and greater transparency with stakeholders and the media. Years of experience count- less as a guide to the future.

As a result, leaders have to listen more, be collaborative, be authentic, demonstrate trust and humility, and be clear about their values and purpose. Therefore, credibility is hard work and something the women leaders here recognised had to be worked at. How did they achieve this? If we break down the key elements of credibility, we can see how important each is and what is required.

5.

AUTHENTICITY

There has been much talk in the last few years about authentic leadership. What it means is that a person is genuine and the same whether at work, socially or at home. The essence of authenticity is 'to know, accept and remain true to oneself' (Avolio et al, 'Unlocking the Mask: A look at the process by which authentic leaders impact follower attitudes and behaviours', *The Leadership Quarterly*, December 2004). Individuals do this by making sure their inner values and beliefs are reflected with their behaviour.

When we begin our careers, some will feel pressure to conform in a certain way and so they end up as one person at work and another when they are at home. The problem with this is that those around that person are likely to feel manipulated or deceived. When you lead, people have to see the real you. When people see you they feel they can show themselves too. The belief underpinning this is that each of us expresses leadership differently and so authentic leaders are consistently learning to understand themselves and gain deep self-awareness.

The best description of authentic leaders states: 'those individuals who are deeply aware of how they think and behave and are perceived by others as being aware of their own and other's values, moral perspective, knowledge and strengths; aware of the context in which they operate; and who are confident, hopeful, optimistic, resilient and high on moral character' (Avolio et al as above).

When people are authentic they act and behave in a way others feel they can be trusted. They also own up to a mistake or share responsibility for something that went wrong. I asked the question to the women leaders here: 'has failure played a role?'. Almost all said they had experienced failure, but they learned from it. Authentic leaders have the courage to question decisions and support their people. When leaders are authentic, there is no room for ego getting in the way. Instead being clear about their purpose becomes the force that gives them energy.

Instead of using a shallow charisma, authentic leaders influence and inspire others by revealing themselves, expressing humility and trust. In this way, they build credibility. However, this isn't just about character, authentic leaders are able to deliver sustainable, outstanding results and this was clear in every one of the women leaders in this study. It wasn't just about being 'nice' it was about being honest about who they were, enabling them to engage with teams and get the best from those teams. Doing so, they are constantly building leadership in others. Their tenacity to achieve results was remarkable in each of the women where they were making an impact on their part of the world. The women here wanted to make a difference and leave a mark on their organization in a way that felt true and authentic.

The women were consciously or unconsciously using their whole life experiences, including their childhood, to become their authentic selves. This enabled them to take risks and sometimes change their careers. This includes Ann Jessopp moving from being HR director to taking an operational role thus expanding her experience that resulted in her then becoming chief executive; or Fiona Clark going from marketing and PR into teaching. It was how they dealt with a challenge or even a failure that enabled them to become the leaders they are today. Not one regarded themselves as a victim even when their childhood had been a challenge. It was through these challenges that these leaders found their strength and purpose in how they wanted to use their leadership. Those challenges are also what shaped them to be authentic leaders.

Most of the women had children and almost all were married. Therefore they had to not only build credibility but also build balanced lives. Part of that balance wasn't just balancing home and work, but also time for themselves, whether keeping fit, attending networks or reading a book. It also included fulfilling intrinsic needs such as social causes, helping others develop and making a difference in the world. They were definitely not 'superwomen' but well organized and had partners or others around them who helped them have balanced lives while remaining authentic and credible.

In today's world of constant change, complexity and volatility, leaders are required to be adaptable, flexible and agile. It is a world that needs multiple perspectives and values, and, most of all, a world of authentic leaders. Gone are the image-conscious, charismatic leaders of the past and in their place we need substance, character and credibility where purpose and values drive an organization. This also requires openness and transparency which is becoming a bigger part of organizational and political life. The reason for this is because the challenge for any leader today is to gain trust.

Trust

Each year the Edelman Trust Barometer reports a global study and a national UK study around trust. For 2018, the report declared that the world was in a new phase in the loss of trust described as the unwillingness to believe information with the rise of fake news. Previous eras were: the fear of jobs due to globalisation; the 2008 recession; and the effect of massive global migration. Now media has become the least-trusted global institution for the first time. Nearly six in ten agree that news organizations are politicised and nearly one in two agree that they are elitist.

For 2018 the global study found those with higher levels of income and education were the group where trust in organizations declined. However, the most disturbing finding was a world moving in two different directions. There were six countries where trust had dramatically increased and six countries where trust had dramatically declined. The biggest decline in trust was in the US, whereas China had the greatest gain in trust by its citizens. In fact, trust was soaring in China. Looking closer the difference in young people in these two largest economies was a huge contrast. Young people in China grew in trust whereas young people in the US declined dramatically. However, the greatest decline in the US was for those aged 35-54 years of age. In China, income provided no dividing line and business was viewed as the most in need for trust. Whereas in the US it was government that was most in need of repair.

How does this affect our leaders? The report found there are new expectations from corporate leaders with seven in ten respondents to the survey remarking that building trust was the priority for chief executives, higher than products and services. Nearly two-thirds said they wanted chief executives to take the lead on policy change instead of waiting for government. There is no doubt that business leaders could do far more in shaping the future, as can all leaders in all sections of society. For as Richard Edelman says: 'the rise of disinformation is perhaps the most insidious, because it undermines the very essence of rational discourse and decision-making'.

In the UK, trust in business fell while social media companies lost the trust of most of the public with the consequence of the majority of people demanding greater regulation. However, there was an increase in traditional media. When it came to government the majority of those surveyed felt their views were not represented in politics today. The British, it was found, are more pessimistic about the economic future with their biggest concerns for the NHS and the rise of political or religious extremism. However, again there was a feeling that business could fill a void and build trust, especially if it addresses executive pay and tax.

Trust goes hand in hand with credibility. Like trust, establishing credibility as a leader doesn't happen instantly and it's not easy either. As the story from Max DuPree shows, you cannot prove your trust by words alone. You need to touch people by putting yourself in positions that demonstrate your trusting abilities to enable people to believe what you say.

Having a credible leader ensures people have a highly dependable source of expertise, experience, information and decision-making. In addition, the women leaders focused on creating a win-win for all. The world today needs leaders they can trust and this is a real challenge. Can women provide this? If women feel they have to mimic men to get into leadership roles then it will not work because they will not be authentic. Without authenticity, trust and credibility are diluted or non-existent.

I always remember doing a piece of research for the prison service. After visiting ten establishments, it became clear that much of the time we were seeing a 'performance' with the occasional governor being authentic. The difference in culture and outcomes reflected this. Why was there a need to put on a performance? Head office at the time had a culture of fear and retribution. This was affecting people on the ground. Trust was in short supply. Credibility was based on short-term goals. Having a culture of trust comes from the top or centre. When there is trust, people can be authentic.

One of the challenges for organizations is that so many people plateau after a couple of years and this affects their credibility and productivity.

The plateau problem

Previously in chapter 4, we explored the work of Carol Dweck on mindset. Someone who has taken this a leap forward is Eduardo Brinceno. He found data on what successful individuals and teams do that is different to what most people do at work. He found successful people alternate between two zones which he calls 'the learning zone' and 'the performing zone'. This was something I found in the women leaders interviewed here. They would alternate between the two zones resulting in increasing their abilities which could be used to build credibility.

Briceno says that when in the learning zone, our goal is to improve and grow so we focus on what we haven't yet mastered. We recognise that we may make a mistake here but in doing so will learn. When we are in the performance zone, our focus is to do our best by doing what we have already mastered. Here we execute and focus on minimising mistakes. The problem is we tend to spend most of our time, especially at work, in the performance zone so we don't grow despite the long hours and hard work we put in. Hence people plateau. How do we correct this?

In the learning zone, we break parts of our role into sub-skills and concentrate on learning just outside what we can already do, so the leap isn't so great that people give up. This is called 'deliberate practice' and results in substantial improvement in what we do every day. In the performance zone, Briceno found that after a couple of years working in a profession, the performance of many plateau because people think that once they have become adequate they stop spending time in the learning zone. In fact, it is always interesting to monitor this to see where most of your time is – and it most likely in the performance zone.

The point is that people who spend time in the learning zone always continue to improve so it should not be ignored. We must alternate between the two zones which is a challenge with demanding work. It also requires four things according to Brincero.

- We have to believe we can improve, so a growth mindset is required.

- We must want to improve and this is helped by having a purpose in what you want to achieve.

- We must have some idea of how we can improve and use 'deliberate practice'.

- We must be in a low-stakes situation when in the learning zone as mistakes may occur. However, risks are part of learning so we mustn't fear mistakes, as long as they don't result in disaster.

In the workplace we tend to foster the performance zone only and this has an impact on the organization, resulting in lack of innovation and falling behind whether it's mastering new technology or thinking. If your work environment does not value learning then there are other ways for spending time in the learning zone. You can find a mentor or another colleague to bounce ideas off or ask for feedback from others. The most popular way the women leaders here put themselves in the learning zone was reading, meeting others or taking a postgraduate degree. They also made time for reflection through which they became aware of what they didn't know and did something about it. These learning challenges are also what shaped them to be authentic leaders.

Judgement

As a leader using judgement to make the right decisions can be another way we tend to decide if a person has credibility. One of the most common dilemmas is when you have a choice of doing what will make you popular or doing what is right, as Chief Constable Sara Thornton had to decide is choosing a deputy. Using judgement is usually associated with wisdom and age, but a young person is just as likely to have wisdom if they choose. One of the best quotes from Kahlil Gibran's *The Prophet* is: 'if he is indeed wise, he does not bid you enter the house of his wisdom, but rather leads you to the threshold of your own mind.' This is what a good mentor can do.

Wisdom can be understood as good judgement and advice in difficult and uncertain matters of life. Moral reasoning is a part of judgement. Wisdom is also defined in dictionaries as 'insight and knowledge about oneself and the world'. This insight into oneself and the world is vital for leadership. Self-awareness and looking beyond immediate boundaries opens up the world to new horizons and is important for leadership today. To understand wisdom better there are studies that make a contribution to our knowledge. Researchers known as the Berlin Group found that wisdom appears to be a cognitive domain that does not seem to have an advantage such as the age of a person but rather reflects individual and specific life experiences.

In Austria, Judith Gluck, a professor of developmental psychology, and her colleague Dr Susan Black (2004) asked the question: why do certain individuals develop high levels of wisdom in the course of their lives, while others do not? As a result they developed the MORE model that relates to four key capabilities. These are:

- Mastery – becoming a master in important skills and knowledge that is relevant to your organization now and in the future.

- Openness to experience – look for opportunities inside and outside the organization that will expand your capabilities, such as working internationally, climbing Mount Everest or taking a postgraduate programme.

- Reflective attitude – making time to stop and reflect so that learning is part of what you do. You can do this using a journal.

- Emotion regulation – learn to not overreact and make sure emotional intelligence is part of your leadership.

Gluck and Black found that people who develop wisdom use these resources when approaching challenges, and by using them, they develop even further.

Other studies have found that personal mastery was a huge factor, as it is a psychological resource of coping and the extent to which a person regards their life in their own control. It includes accepting uncertainty and the limits of human capacity. This is different to a person who regards themselves as a victim and pushes blame for their life on everyone else.

In addition, Monika Ardelt, an American sociologist, has developed a three-dimensional model consisting of cognitive, reflective and affective. She found that the use of reflection was much higher in people who made wise decisions. We can explore her model further.

Cognitive is an understanding of life and a desire to know the truth that includes knowledge, the acceptance of the positive and negative aspects of being human, the limits of knowledge and uncertainties. This, in practice, includes the ability and willingness to understand a situation, and an acknowledgement of ambiguity and uncertainty in life.

Reflective is the perception of things from multiple perspectives that require self-examination, self-awareness and insight. In practice, this means the absence of subjectivity and projection; in other words, the tendency to blame other people or circumstances for one's own situation or feelings.

Affective is sympathy, love and compassion for others. In practice, it requires positive emotions and behaviour towards others and the absence of indifference.

Adelt also shows that culture affects this model. For example, those in Western culture emphasize the cognitive aspects of judgement and wisdom, whereas people living in Eastern cultures emphasize both the cognitive and affective dimensions. She states: 'a deep and unbiased understanding of life is only possible after one has "seen through illusion" and transcended one's subjectivity and projections to perceive reality as it is'.

Therefore, gaining wisdom is part of the leadership journey. Building credibility and being authentic is a continuum of constructing yourself as a leader. In addition, for women in particular, it also includes how you use your voice.

Finding your voice

Vital for women leaders is to have a strong confident voice. Melinda Gates once said: 'A woman with a voice is by definition a strong woman'. The two fundamental ways of finding your voice are:

- Understanding the language for the environment

- Clarifying your values

Let's look at language. Most people do not realise how powerful language is and the imperative of using the right language for the environment you are in. Think of the great speeches in history. Words are powerful. They can move people to act and make them believe the impossible. The words you would use with friends are likely to be different to the words in a board meeting. This does not mean being unauthentic: it means understanding language and understanding the dynamics of meetings whether formal or informal.

If you ask men what is it that women do in meetings that makes them not take their comments seriously the list includes:

- They fail to articulate their point

- They apologise too much

- They go off on tangents

- They don't back up their arguments with facts

- They sound defensive and take things too personally

- They overstate passion and sound emotional

This is sometimes hard to hear so let's analyse this. What can help women? One research study (Elizabeth McClean University of Arizona, Sean Martin University of Virginia, Kyle Emich University of Delaware and Colonel Todd Woodruff, *Academy of Management Journal*, September 2017) titled 'The Social Consequence of Voice: an Examination of Voice Type and Gender on Status and Subsequent Leader Emergence', focused on two types of voice: promotive and prohibitive. A promotive voice is when a person uses their voice to make new suggestions or ideas that may influence the functioning of the group or organization towards an ideal state. A prohibitive voice refers to expressing concern about such things as workplace practices or behaviours and incidents that may be harmful to the organization.

What is interesting about this research is the different reactions from peers to each voice that influenced whether there was respect for the speaker. They found that people who speak up with a promotive voice were more likely to gain status and that both women and men who use a promotive voice are more likely to emerge as leaders. Therefore, the way a woman uses her voice may influence her social position in the organization. To gain credibility, according to this research women should speak more often about ideas that move the group and organization towards an ideal state, but be aware that they may still not get the recognition as much as a man doing this.

The women leaders interviewed here said they watched how their line managers and role models, who were both men and women, set up and spoke at meetings to get it right. Studies have found that men tend to turn up a bit early, pick the best seat and chat to their colleagues. They also noted that they often came with notes of what they wanted to say. During the meetings men almost always restate what the previous speaker said and amplify it in a way to back each other up. If someone disagrees it can get loud but afterwards the men forget it and carry on and not harbour it for days. Men keep to the facts and tend to be precise. Afterwards men stay and chat – this bonding matters.

What women can do is think about their language. There is a difference between 'I tend to agree' and 'this is absolutely right and this is why'. Or 'I agree' and 'I agree completely because ....'. Or 'what if' and 'I recommend'. The language has to be robust and factual in meetings. All this learning and developing as a woman in what is still a male environment is vital. The women leaders did this and in doing so built their credibility. They were still authentic and had values that kept them on course.

Know your values

The values are the compass of your life whether at work or home or at leisure. I always describe them as the rudder of your boat. When you are on course everything feels right and goes well. If you come off course, it feels uncomfortable as if you are heading for the rocks and not sure how to turn. In other words, values are not so much a head feeling as a heart feeling.

Your values shape your character and this is what people want to see and admire in a leader. Knowing and expressing values is part of building credibility. People need to know that leaders can be trusted and seeing leaders make difficult decisions and judgement calls demonstrates whether their values are aligned with their actions.

When you know your values, you can see what drives you because it is so central to who you are. A way to do this is to write down the five most important values to you personally that might include financial security, family, achievement and so on. Look at them and now reduce the five to three by crossing two off the list. Look at the three left and cross one off. I didn't say this was easy. Finally, which one is the most important to you. Now you know what drives you. That's not saying the others don't count, because they do, but the one remaining is the one that makes you who you are.

In organizations culture is driven from the top and that is why having 'our values' stuck on walls only works if they are aligned with the actions and behaviours of senior people. One of the past great leadership academics, Abraham Zaleznik, wrote that leadership comprises of: 'substance, humanity and morality'. These are things you don't tend to learn on courses but are part of building credibility that includes knowing your values. Following on from this has to be integrity.

6.

INTEGRITY

Integrity comes up top more than any other characteristic when people are asked what they want from a leader. People believe someone with integrity will treat them in the right way and do what is right for the organization, community or country. As an upside, such leaders are also more likely to win the support of investors, the best talent and customers. The best response comes when a leader demonstrates conviction, a sense of justice, character and desire to do the right thing. Even if we don't agree with them, we can't help but admire their character. Each of the women interviewed here were clear about what they believed in and were greatly influenced in this by their parents. So what is integrity?

The definition of integrity is the quality of being honest and having strong moral principles. The link between integrity and trust is unbreakable. In short, it is all about character. The word 'character' comes from the Greek word *charattein* which means to engrave. Character is developed and strengthened not static. We all have made a mistake or misjudgement, but the key is to have the strength to learn from it and try to improve ourselves every day. Introspection and reflecting on life's lessons with humility is how leaders build character.

Integrity is not static and is personal, as it is shaped throughout a person's life and is also contextually determined. It was clear from the interviews that integrity is related primarily to parental role models but is also shaped by others over time, life experiences, our culture and education. It is based on respect and empathy towards others; an approach to life that is optimistic and positive; and, the desire to live a meaningful life with purpose. Through these we seek our personal integrity. What impact does that have on leadership?

Greatness

There seems to be a connection between the challenges a person deals with as a leader, their integrity and their greatness. We see this clearly when we think of Mother Theresa, Nelson Mandela, Gandhi, Mary Robinson and others who have been tested.

Robert Quinn (*Harvard Business Review*, 2005) developed what he called the 'fundamental state of leadership'. It involves eight practices that together build ever-increasing integrity. Each has a tension which means that if, for example, a person spends too much time reflecting they are not being active enough but on the other hand to just act and not reflect means no learning or growth is accomplished. The eight practices are:

- Reflective action – combines both reflection and action.

- Authentic engagement – to be both authentic and committed requires a person to love their work.

- Appreciative inquiry – involves constructive questioning that identifies what people care most about.

- Grounded vision – requires a vision that is hopeful yet not deluded.

- Adaptive confidence – requires letting go of control to a state of learning. A person can deal with uncertainty because they have a clear purpose and are confident they can adapt.

- Detached interdependence – transcends the need for control by being humble but not weak.

- Responsible freedom – a person is spontaneous and responsible and so empowered.

- Tough love – a person is both compassionate and assertive.

86

Quinn said leaders are at their best when they draw on their own values and capabilities, rather than copy anyone else. In addition, leading from a fundamental state tended to happen in a crisis situation and was part of a way of moving forward from it. In other words, leaders dig deep and rise to the challenge. This is a temporary state, as it can be exhausting, but we not only raise our own game, but that of others around us and with practice we can learn to enter this state when necessary and then return to our 'normal state'.

When we are in our normal state it feels like our comfort zone and external factors influence our behaviour and decisions. The problem is that most leaders stay in their normal state which is not enough to deal with challenges or crisis. They use rational argument or positional authority to try and force change. They lose influence and others comply, but the outcome is incremental and often just reproduces what already exists. Quinn argues that we must elevate ourselves as leaders to this fundamental state resulting in others elevating their performance. This fundamental state is when we are authentic, following our own values and focused on others rather than ourselves. To achieve this there are four fundamental shifts required and achieving these shifts raises a person's integrity as well as achievements. They are:

- From comfort-centred to results-centred: this moves us from problem solving and everyday activities to finding our purpose.

- From externally directed to internally directed by clarifying our core values and increasing our integrity, confidence and authenticity.

- From self-focused to other focused by putting the needs of the organization as a whole above our own. By doing this, others give us their trust and respect and we build a sense of community.

- From internally closed to externally open, shifting from being defensive or in denial, instead becoming aware of what is unfolding and where opportunities are. We also become adaptable and unique in our leadership.

Fundamentally what Quinn is saying is that becoming a leader is not about being good at a set of certain behaviours or principles or even tools as these don't make leaders unless there is a deep inner change. An example is the explorer Ann Daniels when she was stopped from achieving her goal to reach the pole. At first, she was angry and upset after days alone pulling her sleigh and dealing with hungry polar bears. Then she looked around at the beauty of where she was and saw it with new eyes. She decided to use her leadership to lead teams of scientists working on climate change that would make a difference to every living thing on the planet. Using their greatness was part of how the 30 women built their credibility and integrity. Most of the time they did this when in crisis or a challenging situation such as bringing everyone home from a war zone or seeing off an aggressive takeover bid.

Leadership is always about character and leaders must model integrity in all they say, do and act. Actions must mirror words. They must also reinforce integrity for everyone in the organization. This is far more than following rules or laws. We may follow rules but it does not mean we have engraved integrity into our character. Like all learning, our integrity is shaped by real life challenges and lessons where our honesty and motive is tested. Each of the women here had faced a failure or difficult challenge, but it was how they dealt with it and what followed that shone out from the interviews. These testing times seem to be part of building credibility through testing integrity. Some leadership scholars called these difficult times 'crucible moments'.

Crucible moments

The concept of 'crucible moments' and their importance for leaders was developed by Professor Warren Bennis and Robert Thomas. A crucible was a vessel that alchemists exposed to extreme heat to melt metals. It describes too a situation where strong social, economic or political forces are causing a severe challenge for leaders that tests their abilities. This can be the heroine's journey in Greek myths or right up to the present with Theresa May dealing with Brexit. What is clear is that these moments are both a test and an opportunity.

When in a crucible moment it gets extremely hot and challenging for individuals, making them question who they are and who they could and should be. Therefore these times are not only transformative for the issue they are dealing with but also for themselves. It is a hard place to be, but as long as it doesn't break you, there is something positive at the end. So how do some women leaders emerge stronger and wiser and others fall? It was clear from the women here that staying positive was crucial and believing they would succeed. They may have a moment of self-doubt but it doesn't last. A partner, friend or mentor can help by listening and in doing so the leader can find the determination to overcome.

As much as staying positive, it is paramount to be constantly learning rather than being swamped by the enormity of the challenge. These crucible moments test us and, through learning, individuals can adapt and try new solutions. This often requires making choices and choices in life are often what define us. What can we learn from the defining moment of the women leaders? Each was very personal and different. For some there was more than one defining moment that has shaped them.

I asked the women leaders two questions:

- What have been their major defining moments?

- Has failure played a role?

Shelia Richards, former general manager, Nuffield Hospital

'During the last few years with the second American health company, I did some formal leadership development and an MBA, which included a great section on organizational development. Both experiences began to teach me more about myself and I could see that my Dad's behaviour had certainly made an impression on me. Also that I needed to unlearn some of my ways of being, for example, appearing stand-offish, no time for chat, a workaholic.

'I learned about Stephen Covey and his habits. They made quite an impression on me in my 40s and I still think of them today: that is, try to understand what others are thinking; think about the impact you have on people and situations; change your perspective from time to time; see the other person's point of view.'

Dara Deering, executive director, KBC Bank Ireland

'There were two defining moments for me. The first was doing an MBA. I didn't have a career plan, but it solidified my career and skills. I worked with big egos in financial services and the studies took me out of my comfort zone and stretched me. My second defining moment was joining KBC in 2012. It was a corporate bank and I joined to develop a retail strategy. There was no blue print so it was an opportunity to try something new. The plan worked.

'I experienced failure once. At EBS we did a launch with the wrong marketing message and ended up withdrawing the product. Although I wasn't involved in marketing, I felt responsible. I learned a great deal from this. We rushed things and didn't give enough time to reflect. I still have a fear of failure. Here when I developed the retail strategy I wondered if this part of the business would stay as the decision was not made till December 2016. The fear wasn't for myself but for others. Would I have to tell staff their jobs were gone? That made me focus to get it right. It kept me grounded and I found it was important to keep up with personal fitness to balance everything going on.'

Anne Jessopp, chief executive, Royal Mint

'At the Royal Mint I moved from HR to a commercial role as managing director of a division, which enabled me to get the role as chief executive. When at Remploy, we went through huge change. It was tough but gave me confidence because I survived. Before, I thought I'd always be a number two. I learned to be resilient and stayed positive through the changes. It gave me inner strength and made me realise I can be ok whatever I faced.

'My experience of failure was at the RAC who were bought by Lex.

I went for the role of HR director in one of the groups. I didn't get it which was devastating. I asked for another chance for the job. This time I did well at the interview and was told the job was mine. I was really good at it.'

Sacha Romanovitch, former chief executive, Grant Thornton, global accountancy firm

'There were three defining moments. I married young after university but after five years my husband met someone else online. It made me question what is true or real? It was a difficult time. My mentor Terry asked, "what do you really want to do?". I set off travelling India, taking a year sabbatical. It enabled me to define life and learn meditation. I came back renewed. The second was when I was appointed to the board to become the lead for people and culture when I was on maternity leave with my second child. The third was when in a role I realised I was putting constraints around myself based on what others expected. It was the recession, so I focused on cutting costs, while another proposal said we really needed to invest. I felt I was constrained and others were not. I had some feedback that changed my thinking to accept that I couldn't change everything.

'Yes, failure in different ways. Not everything you try will work. I was disappointed with my degree result and knew I could have worked harder, which made me feel sick in the stomach. So I learned to take responsibility for the decisions I make, to be honest with myself and question the choices I make.'

Camilla Stowell, managing director, Coutts International

'My defining moments are when I chose to move roles. When I went to Schroders from private banking I applied from an advert in the *Financial Times*. I didn't think I would be considered. When I got the job I realized anything is possible.

'When taking on Coutts International Business, which was dysfunctional, as it moved from Switzerland to London and from 30 clients to 130 worldwide, I created a different culture. We decided to "let's build markets around the world". It was scary but I somehow loved that.

'Yes, failure is part of my experience, but if I make a mistake I learn from it. I had one career move that didn't work and quickly moved after 18 months. I have learned how to handle the delivery of the big decisions.'

Cheryl Haswell, matron, Dilke and Lydney Hospitals

'My defining moments were firstly qualifying then getting my first sister post and being part of a fantastic team. We had plenty of staff to choose from in those days and we had specialist knowledge. You need to have the right team to take ownership.

'I don't like failure but accept it will happen. I have high expectations of myself. I reflect and ask "could I have done something better". I was self-aware early. I could have pushed myself harder when younger, but moving sideways I learned a lot.'

Jo Miller, chief executive, Doncaster Council

'My defining moments were during my childhood – living on the council estate was tough; hard but a fantastic place. Mum had four jobs and believed it was her responsibility to feed and clothe her children. Today I have duty and responsibility and refuse to be beaten.

'Yes, I've known failure. In one local authority I had difficulty with my line manager and left. It was hard being told I was no good. I learned a huge amount including not to be an organizational martyr. Failure is not part of me, so it was very hard.'

Sue Gray, air vice-marshal, RAF

'I've enjoyed every job. We move every two years. I did an MSc in aircraft design at Cranfield – it was hard work. I had wanted to do an MBA but the RAF said I should do the MSc in aircraft design. Another defining moment was the second Gulf War, where I was deputy chief for the helicopter force, making sure both people and aircraft could do the job. We brought everyone back and most aircraft. We were the first across the border, as well as handing out aid. All the training came together. We did it well.

'In regard to failure, I'm divorced and regard that as my greatest failure. Work may have played a part. We were both focused on our careers and moving around made things challenging.'

Jane Hutt AM, chief whip at the Welsh Assembly

'My defining moments include realising I had leadership capabilities when leading campaigns and being a spokesperson for Women's Aid before I went into politics. I built self-confidence as an activist that translated into work. I then did a master's at Bristol that drove me to be an enabling leader.

'When suddenly I became a minister, I had to hold my nerve and recognise the opportunity you have in a leadership role. Politics has its ups and downs and you can receive public criticism. I felt very responsible when health minister to the point that I worried about people's health.

'I did the job for six years then the first minister decided to have a change. I was very self-critical and asked myself "have I failed?". Change takes so long to achieve. But it led to a different portfolio and I developed new skills in building a coalition in 2007 between Labour and Plaid Cymru to form a government. In politics. you don't apply for a job, it is given. I am self-critical and reflective as I haven't secured real change and this can set you back.'

Fiona Clark, head of English, Rashid School for Boys

'My defining moment was moving into teaching from public relations and realising how important communication is, which you can learn through English. I've been lucky. Consultancy showed me what I really wanted to do, so I didn't stay long and took a leap of faith.'

Emma Hall is a chartered financial planner and a fellow at the Personal Finance Authority

'My defining moment was winning an award, then phoning my dad to tell him.'

Ann Daniels, polar explorer and leader of expeditions

'My defining moments started with my maths teacher who made me believe in myself. Then living with my brother during the week and learning to stand on my own two feet while still at school. It toughened me up, but it was good spending weekends with an aunt. Working in the bank was a defining moment, as was meeting my husband at the age of 19 years and living in Somerset where I learned what happiness was. Then having the children and being an anchor to them, not just a provider, after my marriage ended. Finally, doing my expedition life, resulting in now being my best, making my choices and, while I love my partner, I don't need my partner.

'Failure happens all the time – mine and others' failings. The biggest was doing the solo to the North Pole when after 21 days the Russians refused access and I wasn't able to continue. I'd had encounters with polar bears and walked through the most tough environment on my own and was stopped. But I turned it around. I fell in love with the scenery and became passionate about climate change and what is happening with the oceans. That's why I now lead scientific expeditions and give talks. I'm doing something that is useful and help make a difference.'

Paula Martin, chief executive, Cornwall Air Ambulance Trust

'My defining moment was the course at Plymouth University where I discovered I was good at leading teams. In regard to failure, nothing comes to mind except that if something doesn't work you have to do things differently. Nothing really phases me, as I believe there is always a solution.'

Rebecca Evernden, director, UK Space Agency

'My first defining moment came early on going to work in the secretary of state's office which is an eye-opener to government and politics. It was long hours but rewarding work. The minister was Hilary Benn, who was very considerate and human. He saw people as his team rather than play divide and rule which some do. Secondly, I was on the Future Leaders Scheme, which opens your eyes to the breadth of work of civil servants and backgrounds of people. It says "we invest in you" and provides space to think about how you lead. Then joining the Space Agency where I took a bill through Parliament and Brussels, the global satellite navigation programme.

'My failure, if anything, is that I haven't always admitted that I'm overstretched – you need to be open that you can't do five days' work in a part-time job. It took time for me to adjust to working part time – you need to make a mental adjustment.'

Sara Thornton, former chief constable of Thames Valley Police, now chair of the national police chiefs' council

'I have had three defining moments. The first was about 20 years ago dealing with a siege. We stormed a house into the danger with grenades thrown at the officers. It ended well with arrests and no-one harmed. That experience focused me on the risk of the job. I became a thorough planner and like to test plans always asking "what if"?

'Second, when I was made acting chief constable, I had to decide who was going to be deputy. I had to choose between doing the right thing or the popular choice. I was torn, but chose the right thing which turned out to be utterly right and encouraged my colleagues.

'The last one was more recent dealing with the real issue of the extent of which the force failed to act on child abuse cases. We eventually got there, but we let people down by not acting soon enough. It was a system failure rather than individual. We apologised to the victims. Yes, failure is something we have to deal with – they are big learning lessons. Your heart races when things go wrong.'

Dr Alice Bunn, director, UK Space Agency

'My defining moments were gaining my doctorate and leading the UK delegation to the European Space Agency meeting in 2016.

'There was failure too. It was a big meeting. For many, it was a great success, but I was given a talking down by the minister about lack of media coverage, because he didn't get the personal kudos he wanted for getting a particular space programme. But it was delicate. The negotiations were not yet complete which he hadn't realised and it was a sensitive issue in Europe. Others had contributed more financially, so we needed to ensure we didn't gloat. In retrospect, I realised that it was my job to have made that clear at the outset.'

Jeanette Forbes, chief executive, PLC Group

'My defining moment was when the business was two years old. We had to work through a bad debt of £179,000 when a client didn't pay. My credibility was on the line, as we owed the City £90,000. The stress affected my marriage which broke up after 31 years. But we turned it around. I told my employees: "I can only offer you work for today and tomorrow". Every single one stayed and together we came through.

'It could have been failure but in that situation you challenge yourself and I asked myself: should I have taken that work in the first place? I later found out that the client had done this before to someone else.'

Diane Savory, former chief operating officer, Superdry and now chair at GFirst

'My defining moment was realising I was good at what I do. I love people and nurturing them and have an open-door policy. I also enjoy joining the dots. Cult Clothing expanded to Super Dry. We decided to float Super Dry on the stock market. I went with our founder, Julian, to London. We watched the shares increase and both cried. I then realised my journey with Superdry was at an end after 22 years. The culture was now remote management.'

Dr Rabinder Buttar, chief executive and chair, Clintec International

'My defining moments came about when the company was just me and I went back to the Japanese company I'd worked for to explore establishing a European market, but they said no as they only dealt with big companies and I was too small. Sixteen years later, I pitched against them and that felt good. I would also add winning awards for Scotland, which is recognition for the hard work in building an international company, especially as a woman in a male-dominated field.

'Twice I have experienced not failure but very challenging times. I helped a company that was closing down by taking on business and building a new office. Eighteen months later they dropped me and built their own office which resulted in me having a redundant office. Also, some companies only give contracts to big companies, so you are always having to build and watch the finances. You have to be strong and confident and believe in the company to do better.'

Fiona Driscoll, former chief executive of global companies, now a non-executive director at UK Research & Innovation and the Nuffield Trust

'My first defining moment was in my first role as chief executive working with Tim Bell at CoBell on privatisations. He trusted me to do them. Then as chief executive at Ogilvy, there were more women and I realised for the first time that not everyone wanted to be chief executive and not everyone could lead.

'Experienced failure? Yes, absolutely. Should I have gone portfolio with non-executive roles so early and stayed in the corporate world longer? It's about our choices. Did I take the right fork? There were fewer women then.'

Kully Thiarai, director, National Theatre Wales

'My defining moments began when I was made artistic director of Red Ladder theatre group, as so few women of colour were doing this. Working with young people I knew what I wanted to achieve. This was followed by becoming co-director of Leicester Haymarket. My next role and defining moment was working in Doncaster where we had £22m to develop cultural space, but with low engagement in the arts. Yet we managed to get more people through the door, making a cultural living room that showed the possibilities of communicating with the community. How to create opportunity for as many as possible has been my leadership journey.

'Failure has been part of that. Rejection can make you push harder, but can also reinforce the voice that says "you are a working-class girl". It hurts when you fail because you know you've had to fight cultural context. Fight for the right to be seen because of your colour. You have to appear confident even when you're not. I'm a harsh self-critic, always seeking improvement in performances on stage.'

Jackie Royall, managing director, Viscose Closures

'My defining moments include being made Welsh Woman of the Year for my business achievements working in manufacturing. It's also been learning that it is all about people and learning. Learning that success comes not from being perfect, but being open to learn, network and be resilient. It was also defining in learning to manage my ego when I move from unconsciously incompetent to consciously competent.

'Failure has been part of it, but it is a learning opportunity. I think the great learning I had from Six Sigma and lean manufacturing is that the feedback loop is to be learnt from every situation and that helped me.

Lisa Marie Brown, managing director, Pinkinspiration

'My defining moments have come from running Pinkspiration and using an impact statement that showed we had helped around 7000 people into work and put £1.2m back into the economy while making a real difference to people's lives. When I bought my pink Maserati, it went online with 35,000 comments. It was challenging and the first time I'd ever had a negative response. My failure has been sometimes managing people's expectations, including family.'

Katherine Bennett OBE, senior vice-president, Airbus

'My defining moments began at Vauxhall where I had to deal with the closure of the factory and was the external face. The decision was made by the parent company just before Christmas. It affected many in Luton who were not affluent. I was shouted at by people and the unions and, at first, took it personally. Then one day, driving home I told myself that this was professional business not family. Today I still remember that road and am having to do the similar things now over Brexit.

'The other challenge in my career was the decision to go to Toulouse where I would commute every Monday and didn't see my husband all week feeling lonely at first. Then friends at Airbus Toulouse helped, including one with who I had supper and the children every Tuesday evening. When other women are on their own somewhere, I recommend going to the theatre, as once you sit down, people talk.

'My failure was that I was made redundant from my first job when the parent company decided to reduce costs. At the last one in, it was half expected. However, the way it was done was horrid. I really enjoyed the work in a large PR company, so when I was called in, I actually burst into tears. But I found another job with a PR firm, then the first one asked me back. The tears made them realize how important the job was to me. I returned after negotiating a higher salary. The experience made me reflect and I retook my A levels to get higher grades.

'Recently, my advice was not taken and it became a personal attack. I sat in my garden and decided to stand firm. My advice to anyone starting out in PR is to go in-house first as you learn so much, such as using timesheets and what takes time with clients.'

Nicola Henderson, youngest ever skipper, Clipper Round the World Race

'The first defining moment was going to a friend's birthday party at about six years of age. I wanted to wear a really pretty dress though I was told it wasn't what others would be wearing, but insisted. I walked in and realized 'this is a really bad idea', but stuck with it. I learned that you must be who you are, not what you wear. It was the same with choosing not to do to university. Everyone told me I should go to Oxbridge and at the time it felt like failure that I didn't. The second defining moment was my first Atlantic crossing at the age of 20. Now I'm the youngest person to have skippered a boat in a Round the World Yacht Race.'

Jenny Tooth OBE, chief executive, Business Angels Association

'My defining moment was to move from PR to economics. I was at the LSE which at the time was very politically active. It gave me a different perspective, a harder edge as I became more politically aware. Although I didn't agree with her, I did admire Mrs Thatcher. She was a force, but I hated her politics. My focus on small business came out of this.

'I became involved in European politics living in Brussels. I ended up with a database of public-sector clients, whereas I really wanted to work with private entrepreneurs. So it wasn't a failure, but I had to start this business again. That was a challenge.

'Building integrity is something a leader has to be aware of all the time. As a woman, part of that integrity is being honest with yourself and the demands of family.'

Integrity of work and motherhood

Just over two-thirds of the women leaders interviewed had children. Most of these had two children, two had three and two had four. There is no doubt they felt the pressure to return to work to enable them to stay in the place on the ladder they had carved out. Each had their own way of dealing with this. One stayed in touch by having her team meet once a month and brief her. For a couple of others, fathers stayed at home. While for some, grandparents were the source of steady family life. As mothers, feelings of guilt are never far away but does having a career affect children's wellbeing?

Some new research by Stewart Friedman, a professor at Wharton in the US, has found some really helpful insights. It was found that for both mothers and fathers the children's emotional health was higher when parents believed family should come first regardless of how much time was spent working. In fact, it was found that children are better off when parents enjoyed work as a source of creativity and challenge. Children were more likely to show behavioural problems if their fathers were too involved psychologically in their careers to the extent that it interfered with family time. This included time on digital devices and was linked to children having emotional and behavioural problems. But when fathers are performing well at work and feeling good about work, children demonstrated fewer problems.

For mothers, having authority at work was associated with healthier children. In fact it appears that children benefit if their mothers have control over what happens to them when they are working. In addition, mothers spending time on themselves rather than doing housework, was associated with positive outcomes for children. Therefore, this research shows that the issue isn't whether mothers and fathers should be at home, as to what they do when they are at home or during work hours.

Therefore if women have demanding careers and wonder if this will affect the wellbeing of their children then they should make themselves available physically and psychologically in quality time that does not necessarily mean more hours with them. This means that when at home not being on phones and spending time on housework which can be outsourced. This information is crucial when lives of work and family are more intertwined. What also kept being mentioned by the women leaders was resilience.

Resilience

Resilience has become a popular concept recently as employees are asked to do more with less in the post-downsizing era. As such we use the word in our everyday language in a way that is not always correct. To clarify, resilience comes from the Latin word *'resili'* which means the ability to spring back. Hence in science resilience is the ability of a material to return to its original state after being bent or stretched. You can see this in a pole vault as it is used for someone to jump over a high bar.

In human beings resilience is part of what we have discussed in dealing with crucible moments. The best description is from a friend and colleague, Dr Carole Pemberton, an expert on resilience who has written the book *Resilience: A practical guide for coaches*. She describes resilience as: 'the capacity to remain flexible in our thoughts, feelings and behaviours when faced by a life disruption, or extended periods of pressure, so that we emerge from difficulty stronger, wiser and more able'. As with crucible moments, individuals are learning and reflecting, as well as dealing with the situation and staying positive. From the crucible, a woman emerges transformed and anew.

The good news is that resilience can be learned. Something these women leaders realised was that leadership is not necessarily a lonely place and each found talking helpful. For some it was with a mentor; for others a loved one or friends; and for one her horses. What each did was for a moment step out of their leader role and connect with others, giving themselves perspective and the ability to see what was invisible.

It recharged their emotional literacy too. They understand their own emotions, listen to others and express emotions productively, improving the quality of how they express their leadership. It also shows their respect for others.

Respect

The word respect came up often in the conversations with the women leaders. Each made it clear that respect was about giving as well as earning. Power can be attractive and can bolster self-esteem, but it can also lead to hubris. Respect comes from how each individual used their power. It requires individuals not to manipulate or humiliate others. When respect is two way, people feel loyalty and respect in return.

An example of when respect is only based on position is the presidency of Donald Trump. In September 2018, Trump arrived late and addressed the United Nations by listing the achievements of his presidency. He went on to claim that 'in less than two years, my administration has accomplished more than almost any administration in the history of our country'. The response from the UN was laughter. There was no respect in either direction. Those leaving positions of power in the administration write books to settle scores. No loyalty and no respect.

In contrast, the women leaders spoke of the role models they met on their journey and how they respected them and in return were respected. They also respected their people and customers. Thus showing both respect and loyalty which was returned. Building credibility has to come from respect and loyalty. In other words, it is behaviour, rather than just skills.

7.

PURPOSE

'This is the true joy in life, the being used for a purpose recognised by yourself as a mighty one; the being thoroughly worn out before you are thrown on the scrap heap; the being a force of Nature instead of a feverish selfish little clod of ailments and grievances complaining that the world will not devote itself to making you happy.'

George Bernard Shaw

Another visible pattern that jumped out from the women leaders' interviews was their commitment to a purpose. This is not a career goal, such as getting to the top, but more about why and how they want to use their leadership. How purpose differs from identity or authenticity is that the focus is on successful outcomes rather than just character and is part of building credibility. Two researchers, Dr Emma Russell from Kingston University London and Chris Underwood, explored purpose in leadership and defined it as:

> A leader who defines success in terms of the legacy they will leave, the impact they intend to make in achieving both financial and business objectives, and more widely in terms of impact at the team, organizational and stakeholder level. A leader with purpose is concerned to align their own personal values with their definition of success, and achieve

a sense of meaning and wellbeing in attaining their goals.

Emma Russell and Chris Underwood, *HR Magazine,* June 2016

Somehow, purpose gave the 30 women interviewed both the ability to perform at their best while also giving them a sense of wellbeing. In regard to performance, purpose enabled the women to deal with uncertainty and risk in the world in which their organization had to operate. It also gave them energy and a positive outlook as well as ability to balance home and family life. Today doctors have found that individuals with purpose in their lives are less prone to disease.

Leadership purpose is why you are who you are. Whether you are a director, chief executive or entrepreneur, your purpose is what drives you to succeed. At its core leadership purpose is why you do what you do and how. Leadership purpose originates from your identity and who you are. It gives a person the energy and focus to achieve something more than themselves. Leadership purpose is not your job title or skills. The challenge today is that our lives are so busy we forget who we are sometimes. As women we are told by others that we should be pretty, sexy, clever, a good wife and mother. We forget that we have one life and it should mean something. Each one of us is a unique human being, so we should know what makes us unique. We have to know who we are to be authentic and when we know we can find our leadership purpose.

Interviewing the women here, it became clear that their childhood had a lasting effect on who they are today, whether it was a happy one or more challenging. It shaped them, made them strong and enabled them to recognise their strengths.

Research by Herminia Ibarra, Robin Ely and Deborah Kolb in the US found that when women have purpose they can direct their attention to shared goals and what they need to learn to achieve those goals. They suggest that instead of being defined by gender, women leaders should focus on behaving in ways that advances their purpose. Key to pursuing purpose is that it is aligned to a person's values and

106

directed toward advancing the collective good. It could be leading a business to make it strong enough to be sustainable and secure for employees or bringing everyone home from a war zone or police raid.

When leaders pursue purpose, they feel they are not only demonstrating their authentic selves, but others perceive them as authentic too. A sense of purpose enables individuals to go beyond their usual expertise and stretch possibilities to remove fear and focus on action. In turn, leaders can then see who they need to be to accomplish their goals.

However, purpose is not enough if no-one knows it. Therefore, it was interesting how these women communicated their purpose and goals to mean something to their colleagues, employees, customers and stakeholders. It seemed that purpose and leader identity were interconnected resulting in impactful actions and results. While the interviews showed patterns, each woman differed, depending on the sector and context of where they worked. However, leadership wasn't just about what they did, but rather how they did it and how that projected who they were as individuals.

While there were patterns in their early role models, their education and the start of their careers, there was something unique in each. They knew who they were and what they stood for through introspection and made no effort to be someone they weren't. This is hard when at the start of a career, but develops with time. They regarded their lives as a whole rather than separate parts. Their purpose was wrapped up in who they were and all they did.

Einstein wasn't just a scientist. He was also someone with purpose. He wrote:

> Each of us comes for a short visit, not knowing why, yet sometimes seeming to divine a purpose. From the standpoint of daily life, however, there is one thing we do know: that mankind is here for the sake of others – above all for those upon whose smile and wellbeing our own happiness depends, and also for the countless unknown

souls with whom whose fate we are connected by a bond of sympathy.

Albert Einstein, *The World as I See It: Ideas and Opinions,* 1954

However, there are good business reasons for purpose to be part of leadership. In the well-known book *Built to Last,* James Collins and Jerry Porras found that 'an enduring sense of purpose' was the main reason for a few companies to have sustainable high performance over time. But where in organizations can purpose be placed? If purpose is answering the questions: why do we exist as an organization? Why do people buy our products/services? Then purpose should be clear throughout the organization, not just at the top.

Professor Stephen Kempster asks: 'is purpose the same as vision, mission, objectives and goals?'. He argues that there is too little discussion on the nature of purpose and its relationship with leadership in organizations. The research here with women leaders found it hard to separate their leadership from purpose and it was much more then vision, objectives and so on. However, purpose does involve action and in doing so builds credibility: '... the highest good for man (and woman) consists not merely in the possession of a purpose but in the exercise of it' (Howie, 1968).

The challenge, however, is, as Kempster argues, that leaders and followers are hugely influenced by organizational structures, cultures, practices and expectations that drive them towards transactional processes and decisions that are focused on external aims such as sales figures and shareholder value. It is certainly the case that this has suited the management paradigm since the Industrial Revolution, but the world has changed and cultures of organizations are slowly changing too. This will mean that leadership throughout organizations will become more the norm and this should challenge the process-driven methodologies used across organizations.

Therefore, theories and models will change including our perception of leader and leadership. One who realised this was leadership writer Wilfred Drath who saw leadership context as collaborative and regarded it as more than a person but rather a sense of purpose, a force that gives people a common direction. Drath took the notion of a 'tripod' from Warren Bennis and transformed it into three outcomes that defined the essentials of leadership. This was developed by Drath and colleagues (Wilfred Drath, Cynthis McCauley, Charles Palus, Ellen van Velsor, Patricia o'Connor and John McGuire, *Leadership Quarterly*, 2008). The three outcomes are:

- Direction described as a collective agreement of goals and mission. Direction here implies a change from the current reality towards some future state.

- Alignment he described as the organization and coordination of collective knowledge and work. This includes the integration of people, structures, skill, systems and processes to produce collective work aligned to the shared direction.

- Commitment he described as the willingness of everyone in the organization to forgo their own interests and benefit for the collective. People would use their time and energy to serve the shared direction.

One of the benefits of looking at leadership as outcomes is that it becomes practical and can be used as a way to focus on achieving the required results. In the study of women leaders these three: direction, alignment and commitment would sit comfortably in how they expressed leadership. Here purpose is clear and totally interconnected with leadership. How can this sit with our present hierarchical structures and management systems? We can ask practical questions such as:

- How is direction being produced in the organization and its teams?

- How is alignment being produced in the organization and its teams?

- How is commitment being produced in the organization and its teams?

- What is working well that we can share across the organization?

- What needs to change and improve?

There is no doubt that leadership has to transcend our management structures. Linda Smircich and Gareth Morgan ('Leadership: the Management of Meaning', *Journal of Applied Behavioural Science*, 1982) suggest that leaders have a dual role that is also conflicting which is to maintain the order and structures while rising above the formal structures to provide meaning and direction involving the embodiment of purpose and values. This was expressed by Cheryl Haswell when she said: 'I follow policy and do like to challenge'.

There is no doubt that purpose in an organization gives meaning to work that enables emotional engagement, enhanced motivation, both physiological and psychological, energy and commitment. An organization with purpose also attracts the best people. While focusing on profit and shareholder return doesn't provide purpose that connects people and often results in low productivity. Therefore, purpose isn't just something 'nice' but has an important part to play in leadership. In fact purpose and leadership are intrinsically linked.

Purpose can be part of a business community called 'conscious capitalism' that includes the founder of Wholefoods, John Mackey. He uses Plato's ideals of the Good, the True and the Beautiful to describe different types of purpose. He also adds the Heroic which Plato would have enjoyed. These ideals are part of humankind and as such should be expressed across our work too. The categories Mackey describes as:

- The Good – service to others such as improving health, education, communication and the quality of life.

- The True – discovering and furthering human knowledge and the pursuit of truth.

- The Beautiful – excellence and the creation of beauty such as art and dance.

- The Heroic – courage to do what is right to change and improve the world.

Expressing these in leadership is what purpose is about and it needn't conflict with economics, politics, our social lives or working lives. It is the difference between management and leadership.

Purpose should not be confined and this is where women leaders can excel. One of the strengths of women is the ability to bring people together and this can be across countries, as well as across departments. Women need to look outward to where opportunities lie. It's not enough to do a job and work hard. Many go unnoticed, so women have to stand out from the crowd once they have developed a leader identity and compelling purpose. The opportunity has never been greater than now when women look at the opportunity of globalisation.

Working in a globally connected world

For the last 20 years, the concept of globalisation has been used (and misused) daily. While we could say that when sailors circumnavigated the world by sea globalisation began, but something new has occurred in how the world has become interconnected and it affects all of us. This can range from carrying germs around the world through international flights to buying products and transferring money across national boundaries. There are many definitions but let's say here that globalisation refers to processes whereby many social relations become relatively disconnected from territorial geography to the extent that human lives are increasingly played out in the world as a single place.

What does it mean for women and leadership in the workplace? For many executives, globalisation is a recent phenomenon. Most of the executives today are male and over 40 years of age with the majority in their fifties. Their perspective of the world and work will be based on their past experience. While some will have had experience of working abroad, it would have still been with a past dominant paradigm or way of seeing the world. That perspective is now out of date. At the same time, more women are coming into different professions and with it a different way of leading and different perspectives more suitable for this interconnected world.

Research shows how women's strengths are about collaboration and dealing with ambiguity. These are fundamental in today's world. The challenge now is to increase the number of women in senior roles and boards as we know they bring with them new perspectives, improve the bottom line, improve how employees are treated and have integrity. What is often missing in their experience is the global context.

The demand for leaders who can operate globally far outweighs the supply. The World Economic Forum's *Global Agenda Outlook* in 2013 singled out global leadership as one of the world's ten most urgent issues and concluded that the global leadership vacuum 'remains the biggest challenge of all for 2013 and beyond'.

At the same time, the world is opening up for women. Numbers of business and professional women in Asia, the Middle East and Europe are soaring, and they want to connect and do business with other women. This is far more than being given the role by a company to market to female customers. It includes women engineers, marine biologists and scientists – roles that were once the domain of men.

Women are now making a mark on the world and through globalisation can have the most exciting careers. Understanding this era of globalisation, uncertainty, ambiguity and complexity and the general global landscape will give women an opportunity today that has not be seen before. More organizations are selecting women as well as men for the roles.

Global leadership is far more complex than that required at a domestic level and places high relational demands on leaders. In their book, *The Global Leadership Challenge* (Routledge 2014), Stewart Black and Allen Morrison interview over 200 senior executives, including nearly 30 chief executives in over a hundred companies throughout Europe, North America, Latin America, the Middle East and Asia. They asked these executives: 'what are the capabilities of effective global leaders?'. From the feedback the model of global leadership they developed had inquisitiveness at its core. Inquisitiveness is a state of mind, a yearning curiosity that drove early explorers across new territories. This, the researchers believed was the essence of an effective global leader.

Around its core, the model has a triangle of capabilities: perspective, character and savvy. Each of these had two components:

- Perspective is about how leaders look at the world and its two components are embracing uncertainty and balancing tensions.

- Character has two components that are emotional connection and unwavering integrity.

- Savvy has as its two components business savvy and organizational savvy.

This means the best global leaders have a clear sense of what needs to be done and how to access the resources to make it happen. Each of these, including inquisitiveness, came through in the women leaders interviewed. They are well attuned to today's different world and how people, particularly millennials, now think. So, it would appear, that women are well placed to supply the different leadership required for the 21st century in a globally connected world.

Ireland's first woman president, Mary Robinson took her commitment of human rights across the world into office, transforming the position from one of ceremony to one of substance. She also showed courage in sometimes doing what was right rather than popular. During her election, she campaigned in more small communities in Ireland and it took a while before even her own party or the opposition took her seriously. But she went where others had not and in her acceptance speech she said:

> I was elected by men and women of all parties and none, by many with great moral courage who stepped out from the faded flags of civil war and voted for a new Ireland. And, above all, by the women of Ireland … who instead of rocking the cradle rocked the system and who came out massively to make their mark on the ballot paper.

When she completed her presidency, Mary Robinson continued her human rights agenda worldwide at the UN.

It's time for organizations and women to take a leap, creating a future where all men and women have fulfilled lives in organizations that will be successful for the next 20 years and beyond. A large part of that will be through women building credibility through their authenticity, integrity and purpose as part of their leadership. For this they will require courage.

PART 3:
COURAGE

'Courage is the most important of all the virtues because without courage you can't practice any other virtue consistently.'

Maya Angelou

Courage isn't something only men experience. When women were fighting for the vote the campaign became violent and the women were arrested. They refused to eat and the response at first was to force feed them in a most barbaric way. It was dangerous and some went on to live shorter lives. A journalist wrote in the *Newcastle Daily Chronicle* in October 1909:

> I have seen brave things done by men on the battlefield, among comrades, hot blooded, flushed and excited. This was the rarer courage which does its deed coldly and alone. What these women were facing was the certainty of starvation, which may be followed by the torture of forcible feeding – a steel instrument between their teeth, the insertion of a gag and the outrage of the stomach pump.

More recently, it took courage to come forward to announce sexual harassment and rape with the #MeToo campaign. Courage is not a gender issue but something we all face in our lives whether it's making a speech to making a stand against racism or turning round a failing organization. Courage is not the absence of fear, but the ability to conquer it. Where there is courage, there is action.

8.

ACTION

An example of courage in action was the Snowdrop Campaign, when three women used their leadership to change the law in the UK following a tragic incident at Dunblane in Scotland. On 13th March 1996, Thomas Hamilton walked into a school and indiscriminately shot children and a teacher, killing most with a handgun before shooting himself. Small children dropped to the floor in pools of blood while others screamed and tried to escape. Parents around the UK were shocked that such an incident could happen. Yet a few months earlier another man had gone crazy shooting people in Hungerford, England. But it was the image of small children being shot as they sat in school that led to three women from Scotland, who also had children, to begin a campaign to rid the UK of easily obtained handguns so that this tragedy could not happen again.

A few years on I traced one of the women who explained how she fought to change the law through organized protest. These three women had never led anything before. Together with courage and determination, they changed the law in the UK. Here is how one of the women described the action to me:

> Firstly, I must say that we probably would not have had national support without the media, especially the Daily Record in Scotland, which kept the story going when other papers had stopped. So the media are important in such campaigns. The other significant support was

from our husbands who took over the washing, ironing, shopping and chores while we focused on what became a huge responsibility. Every day there were letters to reply to, phone calls to deal with and Saturdays we spent getting signatures for the petition we decided to take to the House of Commons.

The petition was where we started, using a wallpaper pasting table. People came from all around Sterling and beyond to sign it. About eleven weeks later, we took the petition with around three-quarters of a million signatures to parliament. However, we were not allowed to see the prime minister, John Major. Only the parents of children who had died were given that option. Instead, we were left alone inside the parliament building with a cup of tea.

We didn't know the rules of the game, so we just did what we did by instinct and I think this worried some politicians. We just knew that what we were campaigning for – to get rid of the private possession of hand guns – was right. I believe we need more people to get their heads out of soaps and get interested in the world around them.

In Scotland no Tory MP signed the petition, but Alex Salmon of the SNP, Jim Wallace of the Liberal Democrats and Martin O'Neil of Labour did, after hearing the arguments. We also had the support of someone who knew all the technical aspects of guns who helped us enormously in understanding that side of what we were doing. The law changed when Labour was elected in 1997. There was a free vote in Parliament and it was passed that no private individual could own or possess a handgun, though people can still have shotguns and rifles with a license.

I asked her about children being killed by guns in other western countries such as the US.

She added: 'The US needs to realise that the enemy is within. They said during the Kosovo Crisis that they would do everything to avoid one body bag coming back to the US, yet more children are killed in the US than soldiers killed in Vietnam and wars.'

These women did not seek to be leaders but it fell upon them and they acted. In leadership character and action are intertwined. Aristotle explained it brilliantly a long time ago in his *Poetics (part VI)*:

> ... thought and character are the two natural causes from which action spring, and on action again all success or failure depends ... life consists in action, and its end is a mode of action, not a quality. Now character determines men's (and women's) qualities, but it is by their actions that they are happy or the reverse.

In organizations, it is action that defines and determines the character and the values of both the organization and its leadership. In their careers each woman interviewed here had challenges and defining moments, as we have seen. In their later careers they still found role models and inspiration to guide them. That inspiration is pivotal to action.

Inspiration to act

When we explore the meaning of inspiration it becomes clear that it is interconnected with action. Inspiration is described as the process of being mentally stimulated to do something, especially doing something creative. Or another definition is that inspiration has the power of moving the intellect or emotions towards making the connection to action clear.

Learning about leadership continues for each of the women interviewed through role models and other sources of inspiration, often usually from wider in society. These role models inspired them to act while they continued building their leader identity. The influence of others is often overlooked but they have a significant effect on how we live our lives and act. Many find inspiration from a multitude of sources. They each explain where they gained inspiration in their later career and where they continue to find inspiration today.

Jeanette Forbes, chief executive, PLC Group

'My role model in my later career was Sir Ian Wood who worked in the North Sea oil industry and later became a philanthropist. He built his business through hard work. Today I also look at other women and others in the industry for inspiration. Innovative people who make me say: "wow!"'

Dr Rabinder Buttar, chief executive and chair, Clintec International

'Role models came from reading a lot in my later career, including books on Steve jobs and Richard Branson. I liked their thinking and thought that's similar to mine so they supported me in a way. Today I get inspiration from listening to ideas in the environment or from my team. I have a buzzing mind so I get inspiration from all around. I have a younger brother with a different background and together we come up with great ideas for the business. There are also different ideas from the teams in different countries where we operate.'

Fiona Driscoll, former chief executive of global companies, now a non-executive director at UK Research & Innovation and the Nuffield Trust

'Through my board work, I have seen different examples of role models in my later career. At the Tote a couple of board members were terrific. Now the chair of the UK Research & Innovation is very good. As a high official in the Treasury he is spectacularly good. He has a soft style and doesn't need to be aggressive but can be relentless. He chairs really well – I'm learning from that.

'I was brought up with Greek heroes – classical stories that were about doing the right thing and being fair. That is the core of my inspiration today along with reading. Creative stimulation is also important to me such as the theatre, films, opera and art, even staring at the sea and the alpha rhythms.'

Kully Thiarai, director, National Theatre Wales

'With more training I went back to social work in Bradford, where I worked in a team with families of children at risk. It was the end of the Thatcher era: with cuts in the police and social work, it became harder and harder to do the job. Friends who were still in the theatre world kept telling me to join them and they inspired me to take a leap of faith. I applied to the Arts Council for a bursary. While waiting I did some work for the BBC so moved to London. I preferred drama to light entertainment. It was the era of John Birt so the culture was challenging.

'I went back to Yorkshire and received my bursary to train as a director for a year. I became artistic director with Red Ladder for four years. Then a new job in Manchester where I helped to create a new artistic operating model then found I was pregnant so recruited John McGrath and stayed as a quiet associate while my son was small.

'Today my inspiration comes from watching others in everyday life. A fire still burns bright in me to do my little bit to make a difference through theatre, make the place a bit more bearable.'

Jackie Royall, managing director, Viscose Closures

'In my later career, I did turnaround work with struggling companies. Having the skill, courage and resilience to go in, tackle it and get a result through people, I earned a good reputation. I went into all sorts of sectors and businesses. You have to learn quickly. This gave me confidence that you don't need to know everything. You just need to learn and have a network of people who you can ask for advice. It is about being resourceful and logical, not being perfect and 100 percent informed.

Every job I have ever done, I thought I would never learn as much again, which has never been true. I have continued to learn at an exponential rate. Today I get my inspiration from books, seminars, watching others, talking out loud. I especially like models and frameworks that allow concepts and thoughts to be shared with others.'

Jane Hutt AM, chief whip at the Welsh Assembly

'My inspiration comes from reading and meeting people. As a politician I am always engaged with people and feel a sense of responsibility. I admire true grassroots people.'

Katherine Bennett OBE, senior vice-president, Airbus

'I still observe behaviour and try to emulate good things. There have been several good examples in Airbus since I joined in 2004. This included spending time in the US, shadowing a lobbying team in Washington for a month. I have had 21 interns and often learn from them. They have gone on to amazing careers. Although I am the most senior person, I like to work with the other senior executives. For inspiration, I went to the Hay Festival this year and lots of talks there. I'd like to do more of that. Ronald Regan used quotes. I'd like to write down more and reflect on them.'

Tanni Grey Thompson, Paralympian, now baroness in the House of Lords

'Now retired from athletics, my work is in the House of Lords and being mother to my daughter.

Here people listen to you. They may not agree but they do listen. But I miss having triceps! When I first arrived, the average age in the Lords was 69 and I was just 40. Here I work on welfare reform, women, disability rights, domestic violence and legal aid. My grandfather used to say in Welsh: "aim high, even if you hit a cabbage". As a crossbencher, I'm not being told what to do, but I have an opinion on everything. People are nicer than in sports. But sport taught me resilience. Our job in government isn't to run the country but to ask "are you really sure this is what you want to do?". I'm inspired by some of the people there.'

Nicola Henderson, youngest ever skipper,
Clipper Round the World Race

'I carried on sailing which is what I enjoyed. On the Clipper Round the World Race I wanted a motto for the team to explain how we'd approach everything. "Doing the best" was ok but not enough. So we went for "doing it with style", which meant we did everything properly and with an edge. We had all ages and nationalities, but sailing is a great leveller, as everyone has to do everything and we should not put people into categories. I get inspiration from nature and where I live, as well as art and architecture. Also people are inspirational, in particular, the little bits of them I meet every day – kindness, generosity and so on.'

Dara Deering, executive director, KBC Bank Ireland

'When I worked at the Education Building Society (that was later bought by Allied Irish Bank), the chief executive strongly believed in higher education and kept at me to do an MBA. It took a few years but I did it. Today I'm inspired by people. I hate being on the top floor, so I go down to see them. I read a huge amount and listen to others. I spend lots of time looking at successful organizations and finding what we can learn from them.'

Emma Hall is a chartered financial planner and
a fellow at the Personal Finance Authority

'I get my inspiration from life – reading books, watching documentaries, seeing what's out there to go and get. Watching an old couple still holding hands inspires me to be happy in life.'

Camilla Stowell, managing director, Coutts International

'Later in my career I had a female boss who taught me the value of patience and the power of personality. I had been at Schroders for seven years and needed a different challenge. I had a call to work for Coutts, so had a look, talked to people and applied. We grew its private office for high net worth individuals, which was hugely contentious. I had to work in a different culture and found your voice is louder as you progress. I had to prove myself but was well supported. My boss Duncan MacIntyre was great at helping me develop emotional intelligence. I didn't think of gender at this stage. Instead, I thought that if I worked hard it was enough. I didn't do politics. I also learned that it is a sign of strength not weakness to ask for help. Duncan made me feel comfortable with myself. I came out seven years ago and am now happy with my wife.

'Today my inspiration comes from clients. They remind me of why I do this. Also talking to people and sitting amongst my team. I'm quite introvert. In my role, I have to network and attend drinks parties. So I enjoy downtime and for this I go running.'

Cheryl Haswell, matron, Dilke and Lydney Hospitals

'In my later career my role model was a matron in trauma and orthopaedics, who was a clinical specialist, managing several wards in a large hospital. Today as matron of two hospitals, inspiration comes from people around me, the teams, from reading and networking. Also patients – one had severe rheumatoid arthritis and painted with his teeth.'

Jo Miller, chief executive, Doncaster Council

'In my later career, Dame Louise Casey was my role model. She challenged others' philosophies and showed that a small group of people really can change the world, the council and each other. What inspires me today is my purpose. I'm a bit of a workaholic. I have a passion for making places and people the best they can be, especially those places and people that otherwise might struggle.'

Fiona Clark, head of English, Rashid School for Boys

'I was at the Design Council for seven years and had a number of role models. Pamela Taylor was head of communications after working for the BBC. She was a natural teacher and taught me practical things, such as how to run a meeting. We had lots of training to be professional. I love artists and how they think.

'I can teach English, drama, history and politics, but because I believe that being able to communicate is so important I have focused on English. Finding something passionate in every child and teacher is my rezone. I love helping others to be better. But we also have to tell someone when they are not good at something as it shows in their lack of happiness.'

**Sacha Romanovitch, former chief executive,
Grant Thornton, global accountancy firm**

'In my later career, there have been four role models. The first was Martin Goddard who was a hard taskmaster but I learned masses. Second was Janet Crook who when she was a managing partner was the first senior woman I encountered. Generous with her time, she was incredibly supportive when my first marriage broke up. She also gave me space to do a pitch. Third was Terry Black who was my mentor when I came to London and he encouraged me to try new things. We remain in touch. Lastly, Malcolm Ward who created a role and let me grow and develop.

'Outside work there is Laurie Young who I met at a managing partners' network. She had been doing global marketing at PWC, then ran her own business and wrote eleven books. She said: "I think you can do something special here, but you have to start killing puppies". What she meant was that I was trying to do too much and that you can't look after all the puppies. My inspiration comes from individuals such as Nadiya Hussain who won the Great British Bake Off and her grace while challenging racism. I also get inspiration from the books I read.'

Ann Daniels, polar explorer and leader of expeditions

'My life changed when I applied to join an all-women group to the pole called Relay. My mother looked after the children. It was an amazing experience and I decided to become a polar explorer. My parents moved into my house and while it meant I was away for certain chunks it enabled me to earn through speaking engagements and so on.'

Rebecca Evernden, director, UK Space Agency

'I took my first senior role in the civil service with the Department of Transport. I joined the Future Leaders Scheme and had good mentoring support. Clare Moriarty was a cohort leader on the scheme and talked about part-time at a senior level. It was on this programme that I met Alice and the role of job sharing at the UK Space Agency came up. We get on well and there is an instinctive understanding of each other and trust in each other's abilities. It's more of a job split and we present ourselves to the world as joined.

'Today I'm inspired by people across Whitehall, for example, a colleague in the ministry of defence is building collaboration between the different culture and ethos of a huge department and a small agency.'

Sara Thornton, former chief constable of Thames Valley Police, now chair of the national police chiefs' council

'Later in my career, more women were joining the police and the first women chief constable such as Pauline Clare, were good role models. I thought "I could do that". They were gracious, intelligent and decent. There were also men around who were good role models too. During my twelve years as chief officer, I have looked outside for other roles models too. I learned much watching the then Home Secretary, Jackie Smith, chair meetings.

'My inspiration comes from reading and I am a magpie for picking up ideas. Motivation is deep inside and makes you try harder.

Dr Alice Bunn, director, UK Space Agency

'In my later career I found leaders, male and female, who resist conforming to the norm of what is expected of a leader which I admire. Women often find themselves in this situation just by the nature of the fact that they are women. The previous NASA chief scientist was clearly a mega brain, but she was also a real giggle, who was not afraid to make jokes about high heels at her own expense. I love seeing men and women leaders who are not afraid to show their personality and it makes me inspired to be myself and not feel like I need to be the identikit- leader that training courses and management books might advocate.

'Today I get inspiration talking to people, hearing about their achievements, especially someone like my sister-in-law who sees beyond her own significant health issues and constantly shows concern and compassion for others.'

Diane Savory, former chief operating officer, Superdry and now chair at GFirst

'My husband and I set up a restaurant but I had no business acumen then. I made a mistake. I couldn't save the business and my marriage broke up. I realized that I had to learn figures so I did an accountancy course at night while working for Cult Clothing. I saw how numbers drove Cult as well as people and systems. So I grew with the business and its expansion to become Superdry and became chief operating officer. I'm inspired by everything going on around me and still learning today as chair of different organizations.'

Sue Gray, air vice-marshal, RAF

'I'm fairly hard on myself and enjoy working in a meritocracy, so being female still doesn't make any difference. My inspiration is my horses – I have to get up early and do my thinking while mucking out. Some days I feel I've done some good – with perseverance you can often get the right outcome.'

Ann Compton, senior partner, law firm

'I think more latterly I have struggled to find people to follow as role models or who have influenced me. There were one or two people I met whilst doing my MBA who said one or two things that have stayed with me, particularly around patience, not getting cross if others are not so fast to pick things up as me, the importance of a sense of humour and, perhaps most of all, clearly understanding the aims and goals before setting out on a task. As senior partner in a law firm that has been invaluable.'

All too often, women leave organizations in later years as they become disheartened to see men bypass them. The later years of these women leaders show that continued learning from all around them ensured that their work had impact.

9.

IMPACT

Each of the women spent time meticulously getting to know their environment and the detail of the landscape in which their organization operated. Whether it was government, the City, business, the police or the military, they ensured that they kept up to speed by analysing their customers, their competition, their environment and their historical culture. They did this by listening, talking to people with new ideas, networking and learning from others. This knowledge became the foundation of taking action and leading with impact.

The word vision has been bounced around for the last few decades. What is clear is that as a leader you have to be absolutely clear of where the organization is now and then define the future. Too often a new leader will come in and decide where they want to take the organization before finding out where they are now and what is working well, as well as what requires improving. Instead of falling at the first hurdle, companies can develop strategies that transform performance. Distributors, customers and team leaders are easily overlooked yet they hold vital information. This analysis takes a bit of time but the result is an effective impact that excites and motivates everyone.

The next part is the execution. This is probably the hardest part and where things are more likely to go wrong. It's also the part that customers, clients, patients and the public see. Even if you are not involved in the execution, as the leader, you will be held accountable so it is important to make sure everything is set up for the best execution of the strategy, the product launch and the outcome. This is where operational excellence comes into its own and as a leader you have to make sure that:

- The detail is right

- The standards are high

- Teams are supported

- Interventions are made if necessary

Keep in mind the impact of what the outcome and result should be, whether it was getting everyone back safely, ensuring the UK benefited from space exploration, making sure customers invested wisely, maintaining services in communities or generating the funds for an air ambulance. The women interviewed knew they could only make an impact with the right people around them, who were diverse enough in composition to stimulate ideas and insights. They also knew that carrying anyone was a weight that would affect the impact of everyone else.

When I was mentoring a newly appointed leader to a large organization he became aware quickly that the problem was the top team. With support and guidance, he acted to restructure and replace them. The top team were individuals who had been with the organization a long time and had been promoted because of that time rather than whether they could do the job. It was also clear that most of these individuals knew they were in over their heads and were not effective. The way this was handled was important as people's lives would be affected. With support from the board after showing the evidence for the action, a new team were recruited. Everyone below sighed with relief as they knew this needed to be done but previous leaders had ignored it. It took courage but the outcome and impact on the rest of the organization was all positive.

Leadership isn't an easy road and sometimes fear prevents individuals doing what should be done. Often we have the choice to:

- Ignore the fear and hope it will go away.

- Live with the fear even though it stops us doing what our heart wants.

- Seek the positive that fear can give us, learning and benefiting from it.

I remember interviewing Rebecca Stevens soon after she had reached the summit of Mount Everest in 1993. She was not only the first British woman to achieve this, but, incredibly, this was the first mountain she had climbed. (Who says women won't take risks?) I asked her 'what was the most important thing you had learned?' to which she answered: 'never to be afraid again'. She continued: 'I faced my fears on that mountain and became aware of myself. I know I will never be frightened of anything else ever again'. Imagine the freedom in knowing that.

Another climber, Jim Whittaker, who was the first American to climb Everest, remarked: 'You never conquer the mountain. You conquer yourself, your doubts and your fears'. The women interviewed, such as Chief Constable Sara Thornton and the polar explorer Ann Daniels, have done just that through their work to make an impact and became role models for others. The decisions they took included changing careers, such as Fiona Clark, taking a new direction, such as Anne Jessopp, or marching to the poles, as Ann Daniels did. There is no more disappointment than when Ann was told she was not being allowed to complete her journey. Through facing her fears, she saw the wonder of the Antarctic and decided to spend the rest of her life helping to save it.

Strength comes from facing your fears. This is why leadership is associated with courage. We need courage to create our personal purpose and vison for the organization. We need courage to challenge the status quo and take risks every day. This is not new for women and our impact on the world does make a difference. The meaning of courage comes from the word *coeur*, which means heart, the centre of our being. Courage then, begins from inside and is a friend available to all of us.

As women we want to be in charge of our own destiny and this desire was described by the American psychologist David Bakan who wrote about how individuals relate to their social world. One of his concepts was 'agency'. It is what motivates us to act on our own behalf, make things happen, excel, experience achievement and influence the environment in which the organization operates.

To ensure impact, be really clear on the criteria for success and your role. In addition, when setting expectations, also be clear on the right outcomes, not just the steps. To have impact, you need to influence the decision-makers. You need to know your boss and what part of the business interests them. In addition, you need to know where to go and who to talk to, so that can help you achieve the impact you are aiming for. This is where your network of contacts is useful.

Network

Impact involves building the right network and being visible. This is something almost all the women leaders actively did. Their networks gave different benefits. For some, it was knowledge. For others, it was being visible enough to be considered for a new role. Networks are more than contacts. Networking is about relationships and a two-way process of helping each other. A network should be focused on both the present and the future. You need to be visible and build relationships that will help your career. However, build the relationship first, before expecting anything back, let them see who you are. The challenge for women leaders is to find the right people, even when they are the odd one out at the high end of organizations.

Too many women have more personal support networks, such as women only groups. To have impact you need a strategic network that is for the future. Creating a network of contacts that will provide support, ideas and insights, honest feedback, resources and information is something leaders must do. Ibarra and Hunter (*Harvard Business Review*, January 2007) found that there were three different but interdependent types of networks.

- Operational – helps individuals manage internal responsibilities.

- Personal – focuses on personal development and learning.

- Strategic – provides insights into new business directions and connections to stakeholders.

They found the least used was the strategic network that is vital for the transition from manager to leader. Leaders have to think of the future as well as the present. Using Ibarra and Hunter's model, the way for networking to make an impact can be clarified and should be made a part of the route map for women who become leaders.

Operational networks

Operational networks enable managers to get their work achieved efficiently using mainly internal contacts and focusing on the current requirements. The contacts are decided by the task and structure of the organization. They can include direct reports, peers within a unit, superiors and others who can either support or block the work. This network may also include suppliers, customers and distributors. The power of this network is based on the quality of the relationships and its harmony amongst each other, but this network goes no further than ensuring a task is completed. This is a day-to-day network that most managers are comfortable with.

Building these relationships is as important as achieving the task, as they will influence the impact a woman has. Remember that having impact means not just delivering but exceeding expectations and the best way is through your team. However, to move towards leadership, women also need to look externally and toward the future.

Personal networking

Personal networking is when your social and interpersonal skills will be tested further as you navigate professional domains beyond your own. For this reason functional networks attract many, but they will not provide different perspectives. At this stage of your career, it is useful to stay in touch with alumni from your Master's or CPD courses. There are also professional associations, clubs and communities of personal interest that help managers expand their perspectives and advance their careers.

For example, in my early thirties I joined a global organization that developed leadership in under 40-year-olds. The local branch had a hundred members from different sectors. We took on huge projects in the community such as organizing Lord Mayor's Day and the Marathon. This was completely different to my day job, but it is where I developed leadership, social skills and new perspectives. I had a young son, but one evening a week was manageable and the contacts you make can last a lifetime, opening up introductions to someone who has the information you need.

A personal network is a safe space for personal development. It is also a place where people can explore solutions to problems and challenges at work. They are external but to gain from them a person has to learn to transform the connections and knowledge you gain to organizational strategy.

Strategic networking

Strategic networking provides broader issues that ultimately open up access to information and relationships to realize personal and organizational goals. The level of contacts in these networks are more sophisticated. Here a person will find the allies, stakeholders and people to help diagnose the political landscape which is part of a leader's role in any organization. As a woman, it also exposes you to decision-makers and where opportunities lie for advancement. You have to be visible to progress. These networks use indirect influence so, for example, a woman seeking a high-profile role as a non-executive director can show her capabilities to a member of the network who can make a recommendation to someone outside the network.

However, many refuse to advance to this stage preferring to stay safe with their present contacts. There is no doubt these take time and energy to develop. Family demands make it a challenge for women, but for those who are constructing their leadership, this form of network is important. It involves reaching outside a person's comfort zone and changing how they understand the legitimacy of networking. You are being authentic, but allowing more than your immediate colleagues to see you. This is part of making an impact.

Internal women's networks

What about the internal women's networks apparent in many organizations? These have their uses in that they can generate knowledge and enhance social skills, but are not enough on their own. For women, making the best use of time is important. Do you have to attend all the network meetings? Many will use the demands of home as an excuse not to network. You have to invest in your career and making time is a good investment, as long as it is the right network. You are adding value if you can contribute more with information or perspectives on problems that no-one else in your organization can see. Some people find leadership to be a lonely place but it needn't be. It can give you huge work satisfaction and it is worth exploring what leadership means at different stages of your career.

Leadership for me

What has the experience of leadership taught all the women interviewed? And what does it mean to them now?

Sue Gray, air vice-marshal, RAF

'It means getting the best out of people. When things look impossible, with a bit of guidance, they can do it. As leader, my role is to set the conditions for them to succeed.'

Diane Savory, former chief operating officer,
Superdry and now chair at GFirst

'Leadership for me means fair play, passion in what you do, leading from the front, being honest and having broad shoulders.'

Dr Alice Bunn, director, UK Space Agency

'Leadership is seeing someone else's point of view, keeping the ship steady, keeping direction and staying unflappable. It is also understanding that if you disagree on some issues, there will still be other areas where you can forge alliance. The 27 other countries are your friends.'

Sara Thornton, former chief constable of Thames Valley Police, now chair of the national police chiefs' council

'Setting the vision, values and behaviours, and being clear about what we are here to do – the softer issues.'

Paula Martin, chief executive, Cornwall Air Ambulance Trust

'Leadership is being in the middle of everything. You take the initial decision, then listen to others and modify it. It includes teamwork, not just empowering others, but creating the right culture and confidence, so everyone can do what they need to do.'

Ann Daniels, polar explorer and leader of expeditions

'Leadership for me is helping something happen – reach goals and help the people I'm with. Get the best from the team. Not necessarily leading all the time, as all are doing their best, but step to the front when there is a need to make difficult decisions.'

Sacha Romanovitch, former chief executive, Grant Thornton, global accountancy firm

'Leadership is acting as a catalyst to release the potential and power of others around you.'

Jane Hutt AM, chief whip at the Welsh Assembly

'Leadership for me is enabling and empowering others to deliver the goals set – the political objectives in the manifesto and enable people to help you do this.'

136

***Emma Hall is a chartered financial planner and
a fellow at the Personal Finance Authority***

'Leadership for me is doing well while inspiring others to do their best
as well. Being a role model.'

Fiona Clark, head of English, Rashid School for Boys

'Inspiring others and making others the best they can be whether it's a
child or an organization.'

Jo Miller, chief executive, Doncaster Council

'Leadership for me is being the best version of yourself. Take the
team to be at the heart of the system and create a sense of common
purpose so that the organization can then be the best of itself for the
people we serve.'

Cheryl Haswell, matron, Dilke and Lydney Hospitals

'For me it's being a role model, trustworthy, honest, fair, visible – asking
what do you think, listening, empower, make people feel valued, be
adaptive – emotionally resilient and consistent.'

Camilla Stowell, managing director, Coutts International

'Leadership for me is delivering through others, building a team and
working together to get delivery so they achieve success. I originally
thought it was about power, but now I see it as harnessing a business.'

Anne Jessopp, chief executive, Royal Mint

'You have to be seen to be part of what's going on – with the people,
not absent, provide support and be prepared to challenge and do
anything. I believe no problem is insurmountable – you demonstrate

the vision, you can always do things and celebrate success. You can't know everything but your team might.'

Dara Deering, executive director, KBC Bank Ireland

'Leadership is having a clear vision, a path and creating a sense of purpose for people to be part of the story. Let people be the best they can be.'

Jenny Tooth OBE, chief executive, Business Angels Association

'Leadership is where I can make a difference and take people with me, bring experience, energy and knowledge to an initiative and nurture others to be a good team. Recognising you have to make difficult decisions and pick up the pieces, take responsibility when things go wrong. Therefore, it also requires commitment, integrity and courage to take a risk. People are what matters – they have to respect what you are trying to do.'

Nicola Henderson, youngest ever skipper, Clipper Round the World Race

'Leadership for me is acting with dignity, humility, leading by example and taking responsibility.'

Katherine Bennett OBE, senior vice-president, Airbus

'Leadership for me is setting a good example and remembering the basics, such as saying "good morning". Being decisive at the right moment and seen to act on it – but listen the rest of the time. Also speaking up and being respectful.'

Lisa Marie Brown, managing director, Pinkinspiration

'Leadership is bringing people with me – inspiring them to change their lives. Using your influence, for example, to reduce emissions by suggesting free bus travel for more people to the Welsh government.'

Jackie Royall, managing director, Viscose Closures

'Leadership for me is grit – determination and resilience. Making time for people whatever is going on. Resilience to work with others despite how difficult it first seems to get them on board. Developing self and others. Making and taking the hard decision but doing it with compassion and good heart. Listening, learning and always asking what we could do better. Prioritising and ensuring sustainable progress is made.'

Kully Thiarai, director, National Theatre Wales

'Leadership is how to bring a group together and make something extraordinary.'

Linda Green, chief executive, Linda's Inns

'Leadership for me is inspiration, motivation, commitment and passion.'

Donna Baddeley, chief executive, Valleys to Coast Housing

'Leadership is engaging authentically with the workforce to do amazing things and it's when people want to come with you.'

Fiona Driscoll, former chief executive of global companies, now a non-executive director at UK Research & Innovation and the Nuffield Trust

'Leadership for me is being responsible for lots of people to deliver that includes a protective role. It's more complicated today with the expectations of younger people. It's about analysis, executing and bringing people with you, but at the end of the day, the buck stops with you.'

Dr Rabinder Buttar, chief executive and chair, Clintec International

'Leadership is being down to earth. Treating people with respect and getting the best out of them as a collective team. It means finding everyone's strengths to build a high-performing team and take them in a positive direction, while constantly innovating and navigating the environment so that you can offer the best product in the world.'

Jeanette Forbes, chief executive, PLC Group

'I'm very hands on and like to get stuck in rather than a them-and-us culture. I like to be one of the team. I have earned respect by showing I'm not afraid to get my hands dirty.'

While each answer is different there are clear messages here about leadership today. Most of the responses talked about other people and teams. The word 'best' came up many times, as well as 'direction' and 'creating the right environment'. Other words that were said more than once were 'listen', 'example', 'respect' and 'responsibility'. Women leaders focus on others, not just themselves or looking good. They are clear about where they are going and how to how to get there. They also know that they won't achieve anything alone only with others. They regard leadership as a duty to achieve through others. There is another part to leadership and that is power.

10.

POWER

Power has always been a part of leadership. The problem is how power is understood. While there are different forms of power from coercion to persuasion, the concept of power is often perceived as a resource that a few have to use over others. Across society power is only narrowly defined as 'the capacity to control other people.' This misconception needs to be addressed as women must recognise their own power.

Each one of us has power, but many do not have the motive to use it to achieve things. Power, like leadership, is a relationship between people. It involves intention and purpose. Pulitzer prize-winning author James McGregor Burns states that the difference is that leadership is inseparable from followers' needs and goals. He writes that while power wielders may treat people as things such as resources, money or tools, leaders may not. 'All leaders are actual or potential power holders, but not all power holders are leaders' (from his book, *Leadership*, 1978)

With our misunderstanding of power we forget about the power of communication or the power of love. By perceiving power as control many reject power as if powerlessness is a good thing. Yet personal power can make a huge positive impact in the world. It can be used to make things happen to improve the lives of others. An example was the power of Mother Teresa. Therefore we should all strive to use our power without taking power from others. This is particularly true for women, who for centuries were disassociated from power by society, whether in politics, science or business.

When the majority of people across ages are asked to draw a leader, they draw a man. This test has been carried out many times. In fact, our understanding of power has been influenced mainly by one publication: *The Prince* by Niccolo Machiavelli written in the 16th century. He describes power as a coercive force exercised through ruthless violence. Regarding power in this way is how bullies, domestic abusers, sexual-harassment offenders and trolls treat others. It also justifies a right for some people to dominate while others are trodden on. In addition, there is a belief that those who are at the bottom of the pile, whether economically or socially, deserve to be there, so we label the poor as 'lazy' and women as 'irrational'.

The classical scholar, broadcaster and feminist, Professor Mary Beard, says power needs to be redefined for women to have parity and be heard. Professor Dacher Keltner has made a huge effort to do this in his book *The Power Paradox*. He writes that we should: 'broaden our thinking and define power as the capacity to make a difference in the world'. By doing so he shifts power away from the few to the many. However, it requires a change in our understanding and thinking about power. Rethinking a concept that has been defined in a certain way over time is not easy. Keltner says that when we feel powerful, the seduction induces us to lose the capabilities that enabled us to gain power. The Greeks called this hubris. But the opposite of feeling powerful is powerless. A state of powerlessness is dangerous and the root cause behind Brexit and the Trump victory. Keltner goes as far as to say: 'powerlessness, I believe, is the greatest threat outside of climate change facing our society today'. By redefining power as Mary Beard and Dacher Keltner suggest, we could transform our world.

How could this be achieved? Keltner says we should: 'stay focused on other people. Bring the good in others to completion. Take delight in the delights of others, as they make a difference in the world'. What is being said here is to shift from being self-focused to other-focused. We have just seen how the women leaders defined leadership with their focus on others. This will require a culture change in the West, particularly in the US and UK, where the culture is so individual and focused on self-promotion. It's been found that those who focus and worry about how others perceive them have less clarity about their goals and are less open to learning from failure.

The power paradox not only affects business but politics too. When we vote in representative democracies we often do so because we saw something in that person to lead. But according to Keltner, it is through becoming leaders that politicians and others lose qualities that were once seen in them. It seems that those leaders 'may be the very people most blind to the problems of poverty and inequality'. This includes those who began with good intentions.

Another perspective of power is to regard it as energy and strength where by coming together and sharing, more is achieved. In this way power is with people rather than over others. To do this requires a shift from hierarchical power to relational power using cooperation, engagement and interdependence, rather than hard competitiveness and dominance. However, this shift varied according to the sector and culture of the organizations in which our women leaders operated.

In a recent study by the Centre for Creative Leadership exploring the form of power needed today and in the future was the power of relationships followed with the power of information. In the past, the power of expertise was used along with the power of information. The requirement today for leaders using their power of relationships is to influence and engage. The power of relationships could reinforce the redefinition of power as making a difference in the world but this would require more responsibility for those using the power of information. Redefining power would also require more autonomy to people to make decisions. This involves trusting people and respecting their judgement.

So, if power was redefined what could be the component parts? The psychologist Claude Steiner has suggested a model in which seven sources of non-abusive power are interconnected:

- Balance – is the capacity to be rooted and not easily pushed out of your physical or personal position. When right it means you know where you stand with all in your life. If deficient in balance, you will be too compliant and nervous; if over-developed, you become stubborn, fixed and boring.

143

- Passion – fuels transformation and brings opposites together to confront issues. However, passion can be creative or destructive. Undeveloped, passion lacks courage, but if over-developed can explode into immense energy.

- Control – is important when in the form of self-control and helps to regulate the other components here. Under-developed, a person can become addicted or slothful. Even worse become a victim and fall down a spiral of depression. If over-controlled, a person will become obsessive and preoccupied with every detail.

- Love – this has the power to bind people together, to work hard together instilling hope and moving out of difficult situations. If under-developed a person will be cold, unable to nurture or have empathy for others or have any love for themselves. If over-developed, a person will spend all their time rescuing others and making sacrifices while neglecting themselves. Love should apply to self, others and truth. Love of truth keeps a person engaged with the world.

- Communication – this requires both speaking and listening. Communication is vital to share knowledge, connect with others, solve problems and build healthy relationships. If under-developed, a person won't be able to learn or enjoy being around people. Whereas, if over-developed, a person can become careless about what they say and not pay attention.

- Information – the power of information is that it reduces uncertainty. Information comes to a leader in different forms: science, intuition, wisdom and vision. The power of information has been misused to control, validate war or impose political and religious views. Today false information has become a real challenge as it has grown and used to manipulate millions of people. Instead, information can be used to enable health, wellbeing, education, wisdom and positive relationships. Lack of information leads to ignorance. If over-developed, the tendency is just to rely on science in a way that can become cold hearted.

- Transcendence – is the power of detachment and allowing the future to emerge without ego. In doing so, a person finds calm and clarity. When we realise how tiny we are in the universe we can even redefine success. A leader here doesn't fear the future. By doing so a leader finds meaning. If transcendence is under-developed, a person will cling to their beliefs and desires no matter what the cost. They will not be able to see the impact they have on others or the environment, because all that matters is themselves. If over-used, a person will become too detached and unwilling to touch the ground and see things as they are.

These sources of power could enable women to transform the world for the better. Would having more women leaders make a better world? Professor Keltner said that at first he didn't think it would make any difference, but has changed his mind seeing what women can do as leaders.

If we explore power then we must also explore powerlessness. With decades of inequality the social costs have been higher levels of crime, health problems, mental illness, lower life expectancy and a rise in nationalism across the world. To gain power people have to come together, to form an identity: examples include the banners 'Women for Trump' or a campaign such as The People's Vote. It's when people come together and think together that power can be restored and this is an advantage for women because of our more collaborative way of leading. This was clearly seen in the #MeToo movement.

Power is a relationship among people as is leadership. We all possess power but we don't always decide to use it. In the 1960s the American psychologist David McClelland identified three motivations he said we all had. These were:

- Need for achievement

- Need for affiliation

- Need for power

These are measured differently in each person. In addition, these motivations are learned and influenced by our culture and life experience. Those with a strong power motivator are divided into two groups – personal power and institutional power. Personal power is about controlling others, whereas institutional power is about organizing the effort of a team or teams to further the organizations' goals. Therefore institutional power and leadership has a connection. However, how men and women practice this often differs. Those who emerge as leaders in traditional hierarchies tend to enjoy exercising power from a distance, but what was noticeable with the women leaders here was their continued actions to bring people together and lead from the centre inclusively. They worked to create the right environment for people to thrive and would actively seek out people rather than stay stuck at the top of a building. They communicated openly when possible and their desire was for everyone to be their 'best' – a word that they used more than any other.

One of the women interviewed early on was at the top in the intelligence sector who changed the shape of the table for board meetings, changing the behaviour of some of the men. She also made a point of having the meetings in different parts of the building so to be seen more by people. When she retired and was replaced by a male colleague they reverted back to how it used to be emphasising the hierarchy.

There is a theory that men and women generally perceive the world differently and therefore communicate differently. Deborah Tannen, professor of linguistics at Georgetown University, gave this explanation:

> For males conversation is the way you negotiate your status in the group and keep people from pushing you around; they use talk to preserve their independence. Females, on the other hand, use conversation to negotiate closeness and intimacy; talk is the essence of intimacy, so being friends means sitting and talking. For boys, activities and doing things together are central. Just sitting and talking is not an essential part of friendship. They're friends with the boys they do things with.

That is why playing golf is so popular for men doing business deals.

Therefore women usually see the world as a network of connections in which support and consensus are sought. Many men perceive the world as individuals in hierarchical social orders in which life is competitive and a fight for success. Men created the business world on this understanding and to some extent expect women to fit into it. Men tend to pay attention to rules and focus on the failings of followers, rather than caring about them as individuals which women are more inclined to do.

Therefore, entering this world that men have built for business and political life is a challenge for women. That is why women taking their ideas and putting them into action is quite hard. It takes confidence and self-belief. However, some men such as Tom Peters are saying that the days of women succeeding by learning to play men's games are gone. He also states that men need to learn to play women's games. This has an impact on organizations and leadership but is the best way to develop followers to achieve their best.

Women need to use their power and leadership now to change the world. When we succeed others, women and men, will follow. The key is to lead the things you want to lead and ask yourself what it is you want to accomplish and why. Know what you care about and what is important to you. Then decide what you want to be a spokesperson for and use power to make a difference in the world. As the advert says, 'just do it'. Identify who you admire and ask why. These are the people we strive to be like. We look for courage, action, impact and power, seeking them in those we admire. I asked the women leaders who they admired.

Who do leaders admire?

Linda Green, chief executive, Linda's Inns

'I admire Bill Gates for coming up with an idea, then having the ambition and determination to build it and make it a success. I also admire his ability to share his fortune around the world to change people's lives.'

Sue Gray, air vice-marshal, RAF

'Theresa May and her resilience in such a tough time. Also Philip Dunn MP who took on a job but not the status and helped us achieve the right deals.'

Dr Alice Bunn, director, UK Space Agency

'I admire Barbara Ryan at GEO (Group on Earth Observation) and her ability to get the best out of people. Also, the headteacher at my children's school who has improved it with her more collaborative approach.'

Diane Savory, former chief operating officer, Superdry and now chair at GFirst

'Jo Malone and all strong women, whether it's running a business or fighting an illness.'

Sara Thornton, former chief constable of Thames Valley Police, now chair of the national police chiefs' council

'I admire people like Susan Rice, US Ambassador to the UN, Harriett Harman, Jackie Smith, Yvette Cooper and women who have done well in business, such as Helena Morrisey and Melanie Richards of KPMG, who are accomplished, attractive and empathetic.'

Rebecca Evernden, director, UK Space Agency

'I admire Tim Peake who went from completing a mission to dealing with people's expectations of him as a celebrity. I admire his patience and good humour in dealing with being asked the same questions a thousand times.'

Paula Martin, chief executive, Cornwall Air Ambulance Trust

'Dan Pallotta who gave a TED talk on social innovation and the charity sector, highlighting that charities should be run by professionals and should invest to grow.'

Emma Hall is a chartered financial planner and a fellow at the Personal Finance Authority

'I admire people who are happy – who have a good work/life balance and don't flaunt their success or wealth but remain grounded.'

Ann Daniels, polar explorer and leader of expeditions

'Someone like Richard Branson who seems to care about the life he lives. I believe he has a soul. Angelina Jolie who has adopted children. "Little" people who do things like swim the Channel for a cause.'

Jane Hutt AM, chief whip at the Welsh Assembly

'I admire the new first minister, Mark Drakeford, and led his campaign. Then there are women in the community who show leadership against the odds, such as Cathy Watkins, who recently died.'

Sacha Romanovitch, former chief executive, Grant Thornton, global accountancy firm

'Kofi Anan. I met him in Berlin and admired his compassion and patience of the world and his ability to see what matters. Then there are those at the Brixton Soup Kitchen who make you look at the world differently.'

Fiona Clark, head of English, Rashid School for Boys

'I admire those who supported me and understood when I changed my career and my colleague Dave who always has a positive attitude, has relentless enthusiasm, enables people to self-reflect, praises others and will have difficult conversations when others would hesitate.'

Jo Miller, chief executive, Doncaster Council

'I admire people who are values driven, such as Michelle and Barrack Obama, Justin Trudeau Jnr and Sue Campbell.'

Cheryl Haswell, matron, Dilke and Lydney Hospitals

'Theresa May – not for her politics, but her resilience.'

Camilla Stowell, managing director, Coutts International

'I admire people who achieve what seems impossible such as Tracey Edwards (sailing) and the late King Hussain. Also I admire people who are authentic.'

Anne Jessopp, chief executive, Royal Mint

'Rather than whom I look more at what I admire them for. For example, Richard Branson – how he's grown the business and the brand.'

Dara Deering, executive director, KBC Bank Ireland

'I admire Mary Robinson – she made some brave policies on topics such as immigration and the disadvantaged, as well as women in leadership.'

Jenny Tooth OBE, chief executive, Business Angels Association

'I admire those in the media such as Kristen Scott Thomas and Helen Mirren, as it's a tough area for women. Also Sherry Coutu who set up the Scale-up Institute and Eileen Burbage who is a member of the prime minister's business advisory group.'

Nicola Henderson, youngest ever skipper,
Clipper Round the World Race

'Anyone who is prepared to stand up for what they believe in and who's not afraid to say what isn't necessarily the right thing.'

Tanni Grey Thompson, Paralympian, now
baroness in the House of Lords

'The person I admired was the Paralympian Chris Hallam, who was one of the most influential athletes in the development of disability sport. He was the first disabled athlete to receive widespread recognition for his athleticism. Chris only ever saw himself as an athlete and he realised the power of the media to change public perceptions. At the time he began competing in the 1980s, the little coverage that existed was generally patronising and saw disabled people as 'having a go'. Chris had extremely forthright views on the management of sport and he stood up for what he believed to be right. On the track, he was known for his flowing blond hair. He encouraged me to be feisty and say what I wanted.'

Katherine Bennett OBE, senior vice-president, Airbus

'Theresa May for her resilience.'

Kully Thiarai, director, National Theatre Wales

'I admire Michelle Obama and young women who do extraordinary things, such as Malala Yousafzai. I also admire women who are invisible, but feisty, determined and resilient, because I recognise this.'

*Fiona Driscoll, former chief executive of global
companies, now a non-executive director at UK
Research & Innovation and the Nuffield Trust*

'I admired Margaret Thatcher – not for her policies but for taking on the world. Thatcher was ground-breaking when I was growing up. Theresa May for her resilience; Lord Browne for his clarity.'

*Dr Rabinder Buttar, chief executive and
chair, Clintec International*

'I admire the Queen. I've met her a few times. She stood for two hours with everyone and my feet were sore, so I don't know how she does it at 90 and stays so calm. '

Jeanette Forbes, chief executive, PLC Group

'Sir Ian Wood, who took his fishing business and changed it to oil and gas in the North Sea. He took university graduates, paid them well, when others were saying he was crazy, and built a thriving business. I also admire Richard Branson – it took guts to be where he is today.'

Who we admire tells us who we would like to be more like. Women have come a long way but the world needs far more women leaders. Our organizations and institutions require transforming to enable inclusive cultures. While parts one to three of this book have focused on how women become leaders, the final part is on how we now transform organizations and show women the route map to be in positions to achieve this.

PART 4:
CLARITY

'Instead of shutting out what is different, we should welcome it because it is different and through its difference will make a richer context of life.... Every difference that is swept up into a bigger conception feeds and enriches society, every difference which is ignored feeds on society and eventually corrupts it.'

Mary Parker Follett, 1918

The focus of this book so far has been on women and what we can learn from those who are leaders. However, the numbers of women at the top and as leaders across organizations will remain low unless the context and organizations transform. There is an important role here for all directors and senior managers. We also have to look at society as a whole from education to the media who have an integral role to play.

This final part of the book provides clarity and coherence on the future for both organizations and the route map for women who wish to lead with purpose.

11.

CULTURE

There is no doubt that organizations are addressing diversity if not inclusion. The two are actually different. Diversity is about differences, whereas inclusion is about developing a culture that enables all people to feel they belong, have the opportunity to use all their talent and progress based on equal opportunity.

There are measurable reasons to develop gender inclusive organizations beyond it being right and just. These are just a few from several studies including the World Economic Forum, Grant Thornton, the Chartered Management Institute and Accenture:

- Blocked female talent is losing the UK over £5bn a year.

- 43 percent of female middle managers feel they are likely to leave their current employer in the next two years.

- The reason they say is lack of opportunities (nearly half) and the feeling that they are being overlooked for progression.

- There are more than two million women working in management in the UK who say that there is a distinct lack of role models in top roles to inspire them.

- The CMI found female managers over 40 years of age earn 35 percent less than men of equal rank.

- While 60% of global graduates are women.

Therefore there is considerable economic value at stake for companies and countries to have inclusive organizations. There is no doubt that the world economy would be far stronger if all these educated women's participation could be improved. In addition, a study of 2000 young people by the UK charity Girl Guiding found gender stereotyping and discrimination is actually limiting both girls and boys in their career choices. One in two girls said it affected how much they participate in school. The study found the stereotyping arose from teachers, parents, social media, television and other media. It also found around 40 percent of the UK population steeped in gender stereotyping limiting the lives of many.

With organizations and government taking positive steps we are still finding gender equality difficult to achieve. What is holding back organizations from being more inclusive when HR departments are putting in place policies and practices such as recruitment on a more equal basis? The answer is that organizational practices mirror societal norms and that is why just having more women will not resolve the issue of inclusive organizations. One of the biggest employers of women is the NHS yet when you look at the top you see men. The issue is complex and therefore requires more than quick-fix workshops on unconscious bias, which, research is beginning to show, actually makes the problem worse.

We are all actively using unconscious bias in our lives every day. In early humans it enabled us to quickly identify friend or foe based on 'are you like us'. Unconscious bias happens in our brains, making fast judgements and assessments of people and situations without us realising it. Our biases are influenced by our background, cultural environment and personal experiences. As we grow up, we form into social groups we feel part of and they influence how we frame our experience of the world: how we see it; and how we judge others and ourselves. They also form our values, beliefs and feelings about others and ourselves. Most organizations were set up and run by men, so the dominant culture is male.

We need to accept that we all have unconscious bias and that it is rooted in our everyday lives. It forms a three-part paradox that we deal with every day that says:

- We are all alike as we are all human beings.

- We are like no other human being as we are each individual.

- We are like some people more than others and we are comfortable with our social identity groups.

All these function together as part of being human. It is a myth to say: 'I treat people as individuals'. In each interaction, our unconscious bias kicks in. Our body language and how we even look at another person will be recognised even if we are moderately suspicious of someone at the start.

Political correctness pushed all this under the table, when in fact we need to bring things to the surface and address them. If we don't every now and then, our true beliefs or attitudes will drive bias behaviours, even when we try to mask them. Therefore, as women we have a choice to acknowledge unconscious bias but keep striding forward or feel a victim and become resentful.

Integrating leadership into one's core identity is challenging for women who must establish credibility in a culture that is deeply conflicted about whether, when or how they should exercise authority. Furthermore, the human tendency to gravitate to people like ourselves leads powerful men to sponsor and advocate other men when opportunities arise. Despite a lack of discriminatory intent from directors and boards, gender bias can obstruct the leadership identity development of an organization's entire population of women. This includes the paucity of role models, gendered career paths and work, lack of access to networks and sponsors, and so on. The resulting under-representation of women in top positions reinforces entrenched beliefs, prompts and supports men's bid for leadership, and thus maintains the status quo.

While there are laws and policies against discrimination we still have what are sometimes called second-generation forms of workplace gender bias.

Second-generation gender bias

Second- generation gender bias is part of society, work cultures and practices that appear neutral or normal but reflect masculine values and ways of working, reflecting their traditionally dominant role. Such biases are so deeply entrenched in our culture, norms and organizational practices that women will often accept them as normal. These form subtle and often invisible challenges and barriers for women based on cultural assumptions and organization structures, behaviours, practices, patterns of interaction and subtle discourse that benefit men and put women at a disadvantage. These biases build up and affect women constructing their leader identity.

With fewer women in senior roles, the result means fewer female role models. It makes it difficult for those women advancing their careers to know how to 'be' in a senior role and can put many off even trying. Second-generation gender bias does not actively intend to exclude or be unfair, but rather creates a context in which women fail to reach their full potential or find themselves excluded from key positions or opportunities. 'I assumed she didn't want the overseas role as she is married with a small child.' Whereas her male colleague is married too with a child, but it was assumed his wife would put her husband's career first.

These assumptions and practices are everyday enacted in an unconscious way, becoming part of the culture in organizations. Without examining the beliefs that underpin them, discourse, behaviours and relationships prevent real change. Organizational transformation requires leaders to experience personal transformational change for themselves, as culture goes much deeper than often realized (as shown by American professor Egdar Schein in the 1980's) and can be regarded in a series of different levels as:

- Level one – the routines, habits, conversations, relationships, behaviours, the meaning people make of the world and their role, repetitive procedures that people are often unaware of performing.

- Level two – the rules, controls, budgets, measurement systems, policies and training that people are aware of as they are affected by them daily.

- Level three – here the focus is on the more conceptual areas of an organization, such as creativity, risk, energy, initiatives, research and change.

Most change initiatives focus on the second level only, while culture change purposefully builds capability for new ways of working. So often what are missed out are the subtle areas in level one, such as the conversations, relationships and habits that propagate the present culture. The outcome is little if anything really changes. So how do you activate all three levels of culture in organizations to address the challenges women face as their careers progress?

Transforming the organization

In many organizations, much of the work around cultural transformation has been put in an HR or Organizational Development box taking them to different stages of inclusivity. However, it only takes them so far, they then seem to get stuck. I have identified five stages that organizations need to adopt to be truly inclusive.

The best of the best are at stage three, whereas the majority are not there yet, although many like to think they are. The key to transforming organizations is that it is led by the top and is on every board meeting agenda.

There are six key areas to be addressed:

- Leadership and their commitment that has to go beyond agreeing to actively address the issue regularly.

- Policies that have to go beyond ticking a box to actively being implemented and monitored by everyone.

- Practices that are addressed if not being implemented.

- Behaviours that are inclusive where people can speak up if these are not consistent.

- Communication that is always inclusive from decision-making to the language used.

- Relationships that are inclusive and not biased in any way.

The personal commitment of senior executives to transformation is fundamental. This readiness is often missed. As often said, you can take a horse to water but you can't make it drink. While there is a huge amount written on change in both academic literature and books for practitioners, there is less written on the readiness for change. It matters because it contributes heavily to the failure of so many large change initiatives, such as mergers or business models.

Ready to change

Perhaps the most well-known writer on change is Professor John Kotter at the Harvard Business School, who covers readiness of change as an eight-stage model with his concept of 'urgency'. 'Establishing a sense of urgency,' he wrote, 'is crucial to gaining needed cooperation'. However, the readiness for change is more than making it urgent. In fact, the readiness for change is a more complex and multi-faceted construct than he states. As well as a shared resolve and commitment, it requires a shared belief in the efficacy of people's capabilities. It includes whether they feel they have the time in addition to their everyday tasks, whether they have sufficient resources and support, and whether they view the situation as right. In other words, the readiness for change is both psychological and practical.

One of the determinants of commitment to change is how it is valued. People will ask: do we need this change? Is it beneficial and worthwhile? The more people in an organization value the change, the stronger the desire to implement it and take the necessary course of actions. However, it is clear that the change will be valued for different reasons across the organization by different people. This can be a challenge but regardless of the reasons, as long as people collectively value the change enough to commit to its implementation, they will move forward.

At a cognitive level, people assess readiness for change by whether they believe the organization has the human, financial, information and material resources required to implement the change effectively. People in an organization share their judgements by asking: do we have what it will take to implement this change effectively; do we have the resources to implement this change effectively; and, can we implement this change effectively given the situation we currently face? This will include people assessing the amount of time to implement the change well and whether the internal (and sometimes external) political environment supports the implementation required. When people share this common assessment, they then share a common sense of confidence and belief that they can implement a complex organizational change.

However, a final point is that organizational readiness for change does not guarantee that the implementation of a complex change will succeed in its outcomes whether its improved quality, inclusion, efficiency or whatever the desired outcome is. If the complex organizational change is poorly designed, or lacks confidence and belief in the change itself, no amount of readiness will generate the benefits. Overestimating the collective capabilities to implement the change is common. Therefore, accurate information, preferably based on experience is far more effective when linked to readiness of change as described here.

Learning is a critical skill for developing a culture that can change and adapt. It does not mean sending people on training courses or singling out individuals for coaching. First, you have to know where the culture is today. What is the logic driving the organization every day in how leaders engage with each other and with others in the organization? Secondly, you have to identify and understand the drivers and capabilities required for the success of the organization. This includes the beliefs and readiness for change. These two are imperative to the implementation of any strategy, so are wider in scope than a process driven by an HR department.

The method I have used for several years is dialogue, introduced by the late British physicist, David Bohm, a brilliant thinker who was emeritus professor of theoretical physics at Birbeck College, University of London. This methodology is excellent when whole system change is required, because it involves everyone and can be used with global companies or large public-sector organizations.

The art of dialogue

Dialogue explores our closely held values, the nature and intensity of our emotions, the patterns of our thought processes, our mental models, our memory, inherited cultural myths and beliefs, the way we structure moment-to-moment experience and how thought is generated at a collective level. The process questions deeply held assumptions, beliefs, culture, meaning and identity. Finally, through dialogue, it tests our definitions of work, organizations and life. It helps people deal with divisive issues as they name and objectify the problem. Instead of disagreeing, people say what they think, feeling and sharing their concerns to build a way forward.

Throughout the process, dialogue allows participants to recognise their assumptions and views in the hope of developing a new understanding, replacing defensive posturing and a feeling of isolation. This is paramount in the first step of moving towards an inclusive organization. It requires all managers, especially middle managers who are most likely to hold up change, and all directors to personally evaluate their world: the change is where power lies in the organization. For true inclusion will spread power and responsibility throughout and control will need to be replaced with trust.

Through dialogue, transformation begins. First, by learning through the experience of everyone else and facing our own feelings. This learning is experiential rather than listening to a trainer and being told what to do or what to understand. Experiential learning comes more from within rather than from the outside. Second, transformation occurs in behaviour through addressing fears, concerns, perceptions and assumptions about ourselves and others. In doing this we address the issue of defensive or denial behaviour.

Dialogue should continue until there is change, though persuasion is not called for. The process isn't easy, so developing the skills should continue. Change is powerful when it occurs collectively and the opportunity arises to work with others in making the transition to the new. Everyone should be involved for the future is created by all people with aspirations, values and growing expectations.

Once change begins it accelerates and is far more likely to be sustainable. It is also a way for people to stay engaged while bringing their differences and concerns to the surface and dig deeper into long-held beliefs that were driving perceptions and decisions. This enables trust to build and by spending time questioning and reflecting, multiple perspectives are generated that can be integrated into the best strategies and leadership for the organization. Meetings also become part of this process changing strategy from the mundane to the dynamic. Dialogue enables people to think, question, explore, let go and regenerate through learning together. For organizational change, learning must take place in the collective.

Therefore, the first stage is for people to understand and learn the art of dialogue in a critical way. These new skills enable a critical mass of employees to embed the new norms of communicating, holding meetings, building relationships and innovating. It is different from just having a conversation, discussion or debate. People have to listen, then together decide the follow-up action. It also means that uncomfortable discussions can take place without judgement as the focus is on the self rather than others. Through dialogue, inclusion can begin.

Focus groups

Focus groups can be used to gather the information to build a picture of reality in the organization. This goes far beyond a staff survey. Remember the focus of discussion here is how work practices are affecting women on an unequal platform. The questions recommended by Debra Mayerson and Joyce Fletcher in their article 'A Modest Manifesto for Shattering the Glass Ceiling' (*Harvard Business Review*, January 2000) are useful here:

- How do people in the organization accomplish their work? What if anything, gets in the way?

- Who succeeds in this organization? Who doesn't?

- How and when do we interact with one another? Who participates? Who doesn't?

- What kinds of work and work styles are valued in this organization? What kinds are invisible?

- What is expected of leaders in this company?

- What are the norms about time in this organization?

- What aspects of individual performance are discussed the most in evaluations?

- How is capability identified during hiring and performance evaluated?

- Added to these should be questions about how people communicate and where; the relationships between people; and where decisions are made and by whom.

From this information you can begin to build a picture of what affects men and women differently and why. At no point is blame attached to anyone in this process. That is why a skilled person in dialogue can ensure that the process is about learning, not blaming or moaning. Honest conversations are opened up instead of staying quiet in case of being judged sexist. It is vital that people are coming together to discuss the culture and identify the everyday practices that undermine the effectiveness of the organization. In other words, this should not just be about equity, but the improvement of the organization in its work and results.

Using and practising dialogue, individuals are learning a technique that can be used for difficult conversations that includes inquiring across difference, self-disclosure, really listening, suspending judgement, showing vulnerability and exploring conflict, resulting in conversations becoming positive and an opportunity to learn different perspectives while connecting with others. This process becomes part of the work culture and a shift towards an inclusive organization. People will take responsibility to ensure the culture is more inclusive.

The information can be expanded with one-to-one interviews where more detail can be explored. This should include both men and women, who can address the beliefs that gender inequality is a reality in the organization in its culture and work practices. Although subtle, it is real and should be addressed.

In focus groups identify what small steps and changes can be taken to improve things and build a culture of inclusion. These should be small steps. Why small steps? Thirty years ago, Karl Weick, an American professor of organizational behaviour at the Ross School of Business, University of Michigan, found that a common trait of highly successful individuals, teams and organizations was the ability to see 'small wins'. He found they keep motivation high, enable people to stay focused and not over-reach themselves. It suits how our brains work. Therefore integrating this method is important here.

Agree who is going to put the steps into action. Again, don't push this onto HR. Managers, team leaders and individuals should all be active. They then have ownership. The actions should not only address subtle bias but also improve the organization. Therefore the emphasis is on fixing the organization not fixing women.

These small steps can be actioned one at a time or in clusters suggest Mayerson and Fletcher. They should be replaced with practices and behaviours that work better for everyone. These should include how and who communicates and where. For example, men in groups around the men's toilet making decisions should be stopped.

Enabling a critical mass to learn the skills of dialogue and practice them solidifies the right communication, conversations and relationships in an organization that is inclusive. It also enables the momentum to continue with support from colleagues, when difficult and challenging areas have to be resolved.

An organization can set up communities of practice where groups can share both learning and success with each other. They can monitor progress and continue to ensure skills in dialogue remain high. These will be useful when planning and implementing the actions required as they are more likely to gain buy-in and commitment to the actions. Communities of practice can help transformation is sustained.

The board should also be involved. As General Stanley McCrystal, when US Commander of Joint Special Operations, said: 'the role of a senior leader is no longer that of controlling puppet master, but that of a crafter of culture'.

Where are things likely to get stuck? My experience of large-scale change suggests that one area is middle management who are sandwiched between the information coming down from the board and information on a daily basis from below. I call this the soggy sponge layer because people here can end up heavy with all the information and need wringing out like a sponge. However, the barriers for women are not just those in a single layer of the organization, but the whole structure of the organization where we work. The barriers are all around women and the best way forward is for women and men as leaders to reconstruct their organizations and rebuild a culture and practices that are not only more equitable, but better for everyone including customers. The aim is to clarify where organizations are and what is working well. Then you can address what needs to be transformed both at organizational, individual, team and department levels.

Once the culture has been addressed, it will make things easier for women to put into practice their leadership. There is still a place for a women-only programme as lifetime bias still needs to be addressed. How this is done is also important along with making it a regular network. Once the organization is responsive, women can focus on the best progression route for them.

12.

ROUTE MAP

One of the surprising outcomes that came from the research for this book was the clear patterns from the women interviewed that revealed a route map to becoming a leader. The model has three overarching themes: construct, credibility and courage. Within these are the areas that define our leadership. Each route is individual but there were definitely patterns.

Early role models

The first pattern to emerge was the influence of role models in childhood. What stood out was the immense importance of the role of fathers. The majority of women had a strong role model in their father who gave them their values and the positive affirmation that they could achieve anything. Teachers also played a part. For others, it was strong, feisty women from mothers to great aunts or grandmothers. Role models are not just people you admire, they are projecting values and behaviours you seek in yourself.

What was interesting was that those with the strong father role model were more likely to go into the corporate world, while those with the mother role model were more likely to go into the public sector. Then what about those who didn't have early role models and school was disappointing? These women dug deep to find themselves and became hugely successful entrepreneurs. Therefore, these early influences do shape us and continue throughout our lives. While this pattern emerged, it is also important to say these are not written in stone, only a strong likelihood.

The women were constructing themselves and their identity as leaders. They found role models early in their career, but didn't have career plans or know where they would end up. What is important is to keep asking yourself: why do I want to lead?

As the women progressed, they still looked for role models they could learn from while being aware that they too were now role models for others. What do you look for in a role model? From those described, some key elements emerged:

- Positive – they stay positive even when facing challenges.

- Empathy – they understand the feelings of others without judgement.

- Integrity – they have clear values and principles that build their character.

- Self-awareness – they reflect on their behaviours and their impact on others.

- Responsibility – they take responsibility for their decisions and actions.

- Humility – they want others to succeed and admit when they are wrong.

- Expertise – they share knowledge and information and continually learn.

- Respect – they respect others as well as build their own respect.

- Trust – they do what they say they will do.

Role modelling is an intrinsic part of organizational culture, yet is often an implicit and unrecognised activity. Both women and men look to role models, as we subconsciously and consciously emulate them. It can be our boss, peers or individuals that stand out for us.

Men look for role models constantly and it is part of their leadership journey too. An example was when I studied the RAF's Red Arrows for two years. The then team leader told me:

> When I joined the Red Arrows, it was a dream come true and during this time I observed a leader who became the biggest single influence on my own leadership. He was very different to most of the other leaders I had observed at close quarters. Everyone respected him; he was always calm, thoughtful, purposeful and delegated well. He made everything look easy and everyone was happy and worked hard. Of the other leaders, one in particular chose to take on too many responsibilities personally and many lacked honesty. Many of these leaders retained their position of authority because they were usually competent aviators – but few had the respect of their subordinates.

We also identify those we don't want to be like and these were mentioned by the women too. Positive role models encourage the right behaviours in an organization to enable greater success. Leaders who are positive role models are a blueprint for the values and behaviours that will hold an organization together especially in challenging times. On your leadership journey, think about yourself as a role model too.

Learning

Learning was a powerful theme throughout the lives of the women leaders. It enabled them to widen their perspectives of today's complex world. After about three to five years, several went on to take a Master's degree. It appears to be an important step not just to put on a CV, but to reflect on who a person is becoming and where (or where not) they want to go. Most enjoyed school, but not all, so we have to understand learning as much wider than education. All the women were learning from every day, every experience and every person they met and they used different ways to learn.

Learning is far more than the acquisition of skills and knowledge.

Learning is a social process. It includes the context and intention behind the learning, through which we create ourselves with others using language and meaning. In addition, there are different forms and styles of learning for which we each have a preference. Two different forms are particularly relevant to those who lead organizations.

It was the work of two American academics, Chris Argyris and Donald Schon (*Organizational Learning 11: Theory, Method and Practice*, 1996), who used the concepts of 'single loop learning' and 'double loop learning' to distinguish learning for improving the way things are done and learning that transforms the situation. It is useful to understand both today when there is so much emphasis on fixing things that often doesn't work in today's complex world. Single loop 'instrumental' learning, while it achieves improvement, leaves underlying values and ways of seeing unchanged. Double loop learning is where values, assumptions and questions are changed.

Professor Ralph Stacey, a British organizational theorist at the University of Hertfordshire, described single loop learning as 'ordinary management' where:

- The directives from the top of the hierarchy are turned into goals and tasks.

- Performance is monitored.

- Skills are developed to fill gaps.

- Uncertainty is reduced.

- We see this in organizations every day.

Stacey regarded double loop learning as necessary for large-scale change. He describes this as 'how managers smash the existing paradigm and create a new one'. This is the learning required for gender parity and inclusive organizations. There will inevitably be defensive reactions and behaviour that will need to be addressed. Women leaders have to understand and recognise how to help both women and men move away from the safe place they know to a new place that they shape through their learning. To manage and to lead are different and transformation requires leadership.

Management produces a degree of stability, order, control, predictability and efficiency. People in this paradigm also run organizations and are called positional leaders but they will find change a threat. Situations such as Brexit will be a real challenge. This paradigm is strong in the UK throughout all organizations. We need to transform management, as Stafford Beer says, from a job title and position to a function of everybody's work.

Leadership is about questioning and challenging the status quo, replacing outdated thinking, behaviours and practices to meet new challenges. Leaders explore new opportunities, not limited or constrained by external forces. This is why learning was so important to every woman interviewed. To master the complexity surrounding them, leaders have to go beyond management methods that are linear or reductionist. Ambiguity and uncertainty demand leadership throughout the organization.

Later in their careers the women leaders still found role models or mentors to learn from. They also fitted in children and it was surprising to hear a couple of them talk about how promotion came while they were at home on maternity leave. There is no doubt that having children changes your life, but it didn't stop the women progressing. They tended to take maternity leave and keep in touch. They also organized their lives to accommodate the new demands.

Each woman built her credibility by being authentic and building trust and respect. They also understood that to succeed a leader has to spend time in both the performing zone and the learning zone. This is a challenge as work demands often result in a person staying in the performing zone until they plateau. Peter Drucker, the management guru, was speaking to a group of senior executives and asked them if there was a lot of dead wood in their organizations. Many responded with a yes. Then he asked them if those people were dead wood when they were interviewed and hired or did they become dead wood? People are not meant to plateau or become dead wood. So it is vital to keep the two zones of learning and performance balanced. With the huge responsibilities these women leaders have, learning is still part of their everyday.

Learning enables us to not only do our job, but use our work to shape the future. Learning enables us to have the confidence to take action and, even more important, it is shared learning that creates momentum for change. While learning continues throughout a career, one of the most complimentary skills associated with learning is the ability to reflect.

Reflection and mentoring

Our lives are so busy it is vital to stop and sit to reflect so that learning is sustainable. Reflection is a critical process for executive women. The best description of this comes from Mats Alveson, a Swedish professor of management , and Hugh Wilmott a British professor of management and organizational studies, who describe reflection as a process that 'seeks to encourage the questioning of take-for-granted assumptions, so to reflect critically on how the reality of the social world, including the construction of self, is socially produced and, therefore, open to transformation'.

Reflection can be even deeper if done with another person through mentoring and is sometimes called 'dyadic reflective space' where the focus is on the interaction between two people with learning as its purpose. This is the work I do with senior executives and directors today with amazing results that make me feel proud of my clients for their hard work. The external perspective drawn from someone else's experience adds to an individual's inner reflection. Mentoring was described by the British writer Dr David Clutterbuck as: 'one of the most powerful developmental approaches available to individuals and organizations'. While organization-led coaching is focused on developing skills and improvement that is functionalist single loop learning, mentoring challenges assumptions and perspectives, is transformational and deploys the evolutionary double loop learning that includes understanding of how to learn. Why is this mentoring so important for executive women?

Ironically, it is often at the most challenging stage of their careers that many senior professionals are left most unsupported. Mentoring enables the development of a broader perspective and builds social capital which is often a challenge with fewer role models and women to connect with. Mentoring is also important because it confronts inner doubts that often result in avoidance of responsibility and decisions – disastrous in a fast-changing environment. However, it's been suggested that women have a tendency not to seek out mentors for themselves, whereas men tend to seek out mentors more readily. Around half of organizations have a formal scheme, but mentors are not developed and schemes tend to be ineffective. It can be disappointing when it is vital to find someone who is passionate about learning and continues to learn in their role as a mentor.

Global research of women by Egon Zehnder, the executive search agency, found that if they don't reach a critical point in their career early enough, they either stop reaching out for support and stay 'stuck' or their organization stops supporting them. The women are ambitious until they reach senior levels where they encounter an abundance of issues. The research found ambition higher in developing economies, including Brazil (92 percent), China (88 percent) and India (82 percent), than developed economies including the US (62 percent), Australia (61 percent), Germany (58 percent) and the UK (56 percent).

The research also found that as seniority increased, women were more likely to report gender bias as a challenge. In the UK it was found that 20 percent of women were not sure if they had access to senior leaders who could be mentors. As they reach the top the ability and confidence to lead, speak the right language, influence, navigate the politics and gain collaboration is vital. Mentoring can improve confidence and performance by releasing the potential within busy leaders when they feel they are at a crossroads. It bridges the gap between theory and reality. It challenges individuals to grow into the best they can be, and that's good for organizations. With confidence women leaders can focus on being more strategic in their careers.

Strategic moves

Strategy is more a way of thinking than a plan as made clear by the women leaders interviewed here. It was how they thought that emerged as a pattern. This strategic thinking influenced all they did, whether it was how they networked or built their credibility. For networking, the women became strategic in ensuring they met the right people who would open doors in their future. Often these would be outside their organization, but resulted in having the contacts to recommend them onto other boards.

We assume the route to the top is straight up by following a vertical career such as accountancy, information technology or human resources. This was not the case. Several moved sideways and broadened their knowledge of the business, sector and industry. Making strategic moves included women in the public sector, but it is imperative in the private sector to become a chief executive, where you need a broad understanding of the business. Many make the mistake of staying in one function. You may start out in technology and move to customer service, then to marketing and finally to operations and chief executive; or begin as a graduate, move to HR, cross to operations and then chief executive. Don't be afraid to apply for a role you would enjoy, as one of the women did when she saw it advertised in the *Financial Times*. Unless you knock on doors they won't open.

However, there are two dangers to be aware of: fear and arrogance. Fear stops us being all we can be. Arrogance makes us blind to what is going on.

To be strategic, fear has to be dealt with. We know that barriers for women are far more of a challenge in male-dominated organizations and sectors, such as law and financial services. However, women with more experience in leadership tasks perceive fewer barriers between their identities as women and leaders. That is why, just sitting and waiting to be recognised as a leader doesn't work. Those who experience dissonance between their identities will try to reduce the conflict and put in place coping strategies such as keeping quiet. Instead, take on leadership tasks and challenges, whether inside the organization or outside in the community.

What often stops us all is fear of not being good enough or being rejected. Someone who turned this around was the writer Marianne Williamson, whose words in her book *Return to Love* were part of the speech given by Nelson Mandela when he first emerged from prison after many years:

> Our deepest fear is not that we are inadequate.
> Our deepest fear is that we are powerful beyond measure.
> It is our light, not our darkness, that most frightens us.
> We ask ourselves, 'who am I to be brilliant, gorgeous, talented, fabulous?'
> Actually, who are you not to be?
> And as we let our light shine, we unconsciously give
> Other people permission to do the same.
> As we are liberated from our fear, our presence
> Automatically liberates others.

As leaders, overcoming fear is part of the job description. Courage is when we look fear in the face and learn from it. Fear can be a teacher as well as an adversary. Fear can be powerful, but only when you allow it to be. Fears are usually connected to and related to our past. The key is not to let the past dictate our lives in the present. Professor Warren Bennis wrote:

> We have the means within us to free ourselves from the constraints of the past, which lock us into imposed roles and attitudes. We become free to express ourselves, rather than endlessly trying to prove ourselves ... Letting the self emerge is the essential task for leaders.

This was particularly true for the women leaders from ethnic minorities. They had really challenging childhoods but fought hard to educate themselves and today are remarkable leaders in business and the arts world. While we all have challenges, it's even more so for women from ethnic minorities as made clear by Kully Thiarai and Dr Rabinder Butter who shared their leadership stories here. What these women did was accumulate experiences that enabled them to build their leader identity.

The other enemy is arrogance which blinds us. It makes us believe we are super human and better than anyone else. What a leader must do is stay between these two dangers of fear and arrogance without being swayed too far in either direction. It was a balance the women leaders were consciously aware of and worked at. In addition, women also have another challenge to balance in their working lives.

Balancing female and male characteristics

The reality is that most organizations are still male in their hierarchical structures, culture, behaviours and language. In addition, many employees still hold the perception that a leader is male regardless of what they might say otherwise. This causes tension between the perception of a leader and what being female should be. It was interesting to observe how the women leaders dealt with this. Top executive roles tend to be male dominated, so the stereotype of those in these roles is male and people's expectations will follow this. To be effective, women leaders have to intentionally show both male and female behaviours and communication. This is to deal with what is often called the 'double bind'. If a woman displays stereotype masculine only characteristics, both men and women dislike her. However, if she only demonstrates stereotype feminine characteristics, they are not considered worthy leaders. Even though they have the same qualifications as a male colleague, they are perceived as less competent. This balance is a challenge and something women leaders have to be proficient in.

The way women leaders do this is by demonstrating stereotype masculine traits with female warmth and care. In other words women leaders need to make decisions and communicate in a masculine way but with a warm smile. This still has to be authentic but has to balance toughness with caring: be demanding of tasks and results but show approachability. Remember Anne Jessopp, chief executive at the Royal Mint, who said that she was comfortable in recognising that she didn't have all the answers but that her team probably did. She achieves by setting the goals and backing her team. If there is a problem, she is available to help. Such women leaders are excellent at getting high performance through people and build healthy leader-follower relations. However, women leaders still have to have one more key element at hand.

Energy

The final pattern that was clear was the energy of the women and how they used it. Their work seemed to give them energy rather than sap it. Energy sometimes appears as a purpose and passion, but there is an even better way. As human beings, we have various desires such as survival, love or accomplishment. Some of these come about from a situation, for example, when getting lost on a mountain or at sea, survival will be a strong desire. However, some desires are independent from situations and these Robert Fritz called the 'dynamic urge' in his book *Corporate Tides*. Fritz describes this as 'an intrinsic desire which is not tied to circumstances'. Such desires are part of who we are and what makes us unique.

The dynamic urge is a genuine phenomenon of the human spirit in which people, no matter what their circumstances, continue to want to create something that matters to them. It is what has driven artists throughout history to spend days on a painting, forgoing food and company, until it is finished. It is what keeps entrepreneurs knocking on doors when they have had rejection after rejection. It is what keeps athletes training every day when they also have a full-time job and little financial support. It is in a teacher who never gives up enabling young students in a challenging area, even when other school staff are full of scepticism. We see it expressed when women have had many knocks in life, been defeated and disappointed and hurt, yet still try to reach their aspirations and goals. It was present in the women leaders interviewed here. This energy is in everyone, be it small or great. This was explained by Khalil Gibran in *The Prophet*:

> In your longing for your giant self lies your
> goodness: and that longing is in all of you.
> But in some of you that longing is a torrent rushing
> with might to the sea, carrying the secrets of the
> hillside and the songs of the forest.
> And in others it is a flat stream that loses itself in
> angles and bends and lingers before it reaches the shore.

It is important that this energy is controlled to some extent or it can weaken the immune system in the body. These women had learned how to use their energy and importantly how to recharge themselves. The women had different ways of doing this. Examples included having time to connect with nature by walking or running, spending time with animals or, as one woman mentioned, staring at the sea and the alpha rhythms. All of these keep our energy or dynamic force in a healthy place.

Being around animals can have a positive impact on your mood and health, either through taking a dog for walk or meeting others with animals. It makes a person consider someone outside of themselves. We know that children with autism benefit from being with dogs or horses, as it lessens sensory sensitivity and increases their desire to connect socially. We also know the calming effect of stroking a cat.

Being in nature, out walking for example, reduces anger, fear and stress. Not only does this make you feel better, it improves your physical wellbeing, reducing blood pressure, heart rate, muscle tension and the production of stress hormones. Connecting with nature also improves sleep patterns and depression. It puts everything into perspective and problems don't seem so huge. As a leader, we must look after ourselves, as others rely on us to perform.

What you are doing is taking yourself from your inner world to the natural world and this heightens your overall wellbeing. We hear so much about mental health these days and some such as David Attenborough talk about how we have disconnected ourselves from the natural world and that we should find a way back. An important part of mental health is to be able to move outside yourself and simply be in the present, conscious in the moment. This enables inner calm and clearer judgement, so the brain can be focused and creative in responding to the challenges of leadership and life. Even if you live in a city, there will be parks or gardens or places nearby that have rivers, hills or the sea.

Being near the sea is also good for us. The sound of waves alters our mental wave patterns. The frequency of sea waves slows the brain from the faster beta brainwaves that we use for quick, intellectual thinking. By listening to alpha waves we move into the deeply relaxing alpha state. Here we use the right side of the brain where emotions, feelings and intuition are used. You become more aware of your body and your breathing. In yoga there is a form of breathing called ujjay pranayama or ocean breath. This is achieved by slowly inhaling a breath for a count of ten, then exhaling for the same pace. As you exhale you will hear a sound from the back of your throat that is similar to water running. Doing this a couple of times will take you to the alpha state.

These are some of the ways that enabled the women to travel their leadership route map to be successful leaders in what is still, though changing, a male world. However, until organizations and society changes the journey for women around the world will be thwarted. What is important for women is to build a support network around themselves and to be clear about why they want to lead.

The exceptional women, who will lead organizations in the future, will experience a journey of discovery and new insights, learning and deep development. They will develop the right mindset and thinking to deal with a world that is ambiguous, complex and unpredictable. They will develop courage, leader self-efficacy and resilience while finding their authentic leadership selves to address both challenges and opportunities.

CONCLUSION

'... human progress is neither automatic nor inevitable; it requires the tireless exertions and passionate concern of dedicated individuals.'

Dr Martin Luther King Jnr

This study began following a webinar for International Women's Day in 2018 and the decision to make 2018 a campaign to promote more women leaders. The research, interviews and writing has been an inspiring journey. It is all the more inspiring when you consider the odds and challenges facing women today. In 2018, only 3 percent of Fortune 500 companies have a female chief executive and the percentage of executive women on FTSE 100 boards remains stagnant at 12 percent. A quarter of FTSE 100 boards are still comprised of 100 percent men. In the background, companies still claim the problem to be one of the choices women make, whereas the reality is a much more systemic problem across society. In all walks of life whether government, the police, science, technology or financial services, women still have hurdles to cross that men do not.

A huge barrier is one of perception. In surveys, most men believe equal opportunity is a reality, while fewer than a third of women do. The reality is that until gender parity is a top strategic action in every boardroom, the barriers will remain. This does not mean implementing rigid quotas or ticking the box by taking on a token non-executive director. Both boards and head hunting companies need to make more effort to find capable women. At the same time, women and men together must play a role too. They must challenge the media, the home, the workplace, schools and universities; they must come together and face the realities and different perceptions, as well of the benefits, that an equal society would bring.

Why is this important? Enabling women to participate equally in the global economy could add $28 trillion in GDP growth by 2025, according to the World Economic Forum. As women devote more of the household budget to education, health and nutrition, so the whole country benefits. In addition, the World Bank has found that by increasing the female labour market, poverty is substantially reduced, although the World Trade Organization has found it is happening too slowly and not systematically. Equality isn't just about getting seats on a board, but improving society.

To conclude I want to focus on leadership as a practice, sometimes called praxis. The best description comes from the Cambridge English Dictionary that describes it as: 'the process of using a theory or something that you have learned in a practical way'. What I have tried to show here is how 30 women learned and practiced leadership in a way that is making a difference today to employees, customers, shareholders and governments.

The concept 'to lead' is derived from an ancient language where the word '*laed*' meant to follow a path. That is why leadership is a journey and is expressed differently by each of us. In addition, a leader is someone who guides those travelling the path. This book has been written for those who are following the path. What became clear from the interviews is that some paths were very hard, especially for those women from ethnic minorities. For certain, the leadership journey will be easier when patriarchal hierarchies are replaced with communities of good practice. For organizations, whether locally or globally, the first action must be to makes themselves more inclusive.

In these challenging times, the world needs leaders who see different perspectives, such as the women interviewed here who are different from backgrounds and sectors. While fathers have played a significant role in developing their daughters as leaders, they also need to work to change the system, the media, organizations, education and society, so that all women can have the same chance of being leaders as men.

Yes, things are changing but not as much as some believe. A recent study of Harvard male undergraduates said they considered their careers to be more significant and important than their future wives who they expect to be the main child carers. Yet I meet women in the UK who have partners who share care of the home and family on a fifty- fifty basis. So where do we start to ensure we have the leaders the world requires? How do we put leadership into practice after 50 years of theories, models and, the worst of all, competency frameworks?

The path the women here followed was one of significant learning that included role models, listening to others, reading, observing, studying, experiencing, taking risks, sometimes failing, building leader identity, finding their purpose, facing crucible moments, building credibility, dealing with disappointments and having the courage to act. The development of leaders in organizations has been focusing on the wrong things. It should switch from tick-box qualifications and skills to focusing on results. Instead of developing high potential, identify those who love to learn. To develop leaders, you need leaders who practice it and learn. This learning can be inside or outside the organization or wherever action is required with results that matter. It is these key events or defining moments that shape leaders. Yet many organizations still believe that the answer is the right training programme when it is the experience individuals have and the colleagues they meet to stretch them as well as support them that is more important.

For more women to become leaders, organizations have to transform. This includes providing the experiences that will expose individuals to different perspectives tackling complex issues. Line managers have to become leaders and guide their people on the leadership path. This does not mean suddenly telling them they are now coaches. Instead it is the realization that they are role modelling leadership in their actions, words, values and behaviours, as they continue to learn themselves, while being authentic and trustworthy.

The women in this study have followed the path of becoming examples. Their humility and stories are inspiring. The challenge is to ensure more women become leaders, not for the position, but to use their leadership to a purpose, to transform organizations and change the world to be a better place for all its citizens. As Celtic women once fought for fairness, they and the rest of the world, men and women together, must do so again.

The momentum for parity across the world continues at national, governmental and business levels. The world cries out for women who can lead to make a difference, focus on others and change the world. As the well-known psychologist Carl Jung wrote:

> In the last analysis, the essential thing is the life of the individual. This alone makes history, here alone do the great transformations just take place, and the whole future, the whole history of the world, ultimately spring as a gigantic summation from these hidden sources in individuals. In our most private and subjective lives we are not only the passive witnesses of our age, and its sufferers, but also its makers. We make our own epoch.

SOURCES

- *Global Gender Gap Report*, World Economic Forum: www.weforum.org

- *The Female FTSE Board Report*, Cranfield School of Management, 2018: www.cranfield.ac.uk/som/press/cranfield-ftse-report-highlights-female-under-representation-in-executive-ranks

- FTSE Women Leaders, the Hampton-Alexander Review of FTSE 350 companies: www.gov.uk/government/publications/ftse-women-leaders-hampton-alexander-review

- *Diversity Matters*, an annual report by McKinsey: www.Mckinsey.com/businessfunctions/organizations/why-diversity-matters

- *Harvard Business Review*: www.hbr.org

- *UK Gender Pay Gap Report*, McKinsey, 2018: www.McKinsey.com/UK/our-people/UK-gender-pay-gap-report

- *Women in Business*, a report by Grant Thornton, 2018: www.grantthornton.global/insights/women-in-business-2018

- Geena Davis Institute on Gender in Media: www.seejane.org

- *Creating Leaders in the Classroom*, Hilarie Owen, 2007

- *On Becoming a Leader*, Warren Bennis, updated edition, Perseus Books Group, 2003

- *New Thinking on Leadership*, edited by Hilarie Owen, Kogan Page, 2012

- *Mindset: the New Psychology of Success*, Carol Dweck, Random House, 2006

- Edelman Trust Barometer: www.edelman.com/trust-barometer

- TED talk by Eduardo Briceno: www.ted.com/speakers/eduardo_briceno

- *Leading for a Lifetime*, Warren Bennis and Robert Thomas, Harvard Business School Press 2007

- *The Power Paradox*, Dacher Keltner, Penguin Random House, 2017

- *Women & Power: a Manifesto*, Mary Beard, Profile Books, 2017

- *Dialogue*, David Bohm, Routledge, 1999

ACKNOWLEDGEMENTS

Anyone writing a book will know how time demanding the process is. Add to that running a business and it is clear how important support is. For me, I have had the support of my publisher Adam Jolly throughout. Often with a large publisher it can feel you are just a number. In addition, as an author you have to fit into their 'boxes'. This is hard for a creative soul. However, Adam was able to allow me freedom to explore while making sure things didn't run off at a tangent. Having a critical eye on your work is extremely helpful too. His patience and support has been consistent and for that I am very grateful. In addition, I would like to thank my design consultant Chantel who designed the cover and who does all the creative work for me.

I have also had the support of friends and family. Each phone call they have asked 'how is the book going?'. In addition, my advisory board has been amazingly helpful, especially Felicity, Dilys, Bernadette and Fiona, and, unofficially, Andrew and John. Their passion for this work has been so important, especially on days when stuck in front of a computer. I would also like to thank Brian who has been an adviser and discussion partner for several years. Then there are my wonderful clients including Theresa, Mark and Nick, Karen, Nigel and Emma.

However, while my name is on the cover I could not have written this without the time given by the amazing women I interviewed. They were so so honest, courageous and inspiring. They show that becoming a leader is about becoming yourself at your best. This transformation is a life's journey. Taken together, their experiences opened up a whole series of patterns or themes. Their participation strengthens our understanding of leaders who happen to be women.

Often overlooked are the people behind the scene, the PAs and staff officers, who played their part in setting up the appointments for the interviews. On arrival at the organizations they were welcoming and friendly. The whole experience has been a journey in itself with flights, trains, taxis, long drives and phone calls. All this shows that a book is never one person but the collaboration of many.

Lightning Source UK Ltd.
Milton Keynes UK
UKHW040057210619
344767UK00001B/118/P